Russia's Abandoned Children

An Intimate Understanding

Clementine K. Fujimura

*with Sally W. Stoecker and
Tatyana Sudakova*

Westport, Connecticut
London

Library of Congress Cataloging-in-Publication Data

Fujimura, Clementine K., 1965–
   Russia's abandoned children : an intimate understanding / Clementine K.
Fujimura with Sally W. Stoecker and Tatyana Sudakova
        p.   cm.
   Includes bibliographical references and index.
   ISBN 0–275–97909–1 (alk. paper)
1. Abandoned children—Russia (Federation)   2. Street children—Russia
(Federation)   I. Stoecker, Sally W.   II. Sudakova, Tatyana.   III. Title.
HV887.R8F85   2005
305.23'086'9450947—dc22   2005017476

British Library Cataloguing in Publication Data is available.

Library of Congress Catalog Card Number: 2005017476
ISBN: 0–275–97909–1

First published in 2005

Praeger Publishers, 88 Post Road West, Westport, CT 06881
An imprint of Greenwood Publishing Group, Inc.
www.praeger.com

Printed in the United States of America

∞

The paper used in this book complies with the
Permanent Paper Standard issued by the National
Information Standards Organization (Z39.48–1984).

10 9 8 7 6 5 4 3 2 1

Contents

Acknowledgments

Words cannot express my gratitude to all those who supported the research and writing of this manuscript: The Kennan Institute in Washington, D.C., under the direction of Dr. Blaire Ruble, has over the years supported me in numerous ways, enabling me to research and present parts of my work. The U.S. Naval Academy has also played a vital role in supporting my research, as has the American Council of Teachers of Russian, under the direction of Dr. Dan Davidson. I am extremely thankful to these institutions.

In Russia, I cannot thank enough those individuals who helped me access vital information and resources and ultimately found ways for me to interview and spend time with the children and their caretakers. These include Sapar Mulaevich, director of the Moscow shelter Way Home, Maria from Maria's Children, and many directors from various orphanages in Moscow and St. Petersburg.

In the United States a number of individuals helped me throughout the writing process. First and foremost, I must thank Professor Paul Friedrich at the University of Chicago, without whom I would not be where I am today. Thanks go also to my students and colleagues, in particular Chris Buck, who assisted me in editing the manuscript. I would also like to extend my sincere thanks to Melissa Joyce, editor, neighbor, and friend, whose expertise and patience allowed me to envision and create a work written from the heart.

Finally, to my family, my husband Paul and sons Willem and Tristan: Thank you for being there for me through thick and thin and for reminding me how fortunate we are to have each other.

Introduction: Entering the Doorway to Abandoned Russia

It is the summer of 1992. Russia is in the midst of social and political upheaval. Markets are bustling with activity as people try to sell anything and everything, from homemade clothes made from yarn woven from their dogs' fur to vodka produced in their bathtubs. All this in order to get by in a time when prices are going up while pay is low and irregular. I have arrived at the Moscow airport with two duffle bags packed with children's clothes, diaper rash cream, multivitamins, and diapers. The duffle bags are not for me, but for orphans. I have come to spend the next six weeks volunteering in a baby orphanage in Moscow. After an hour or so of wondering whether I am ever going to leave the airport, I see a tall man, cigarette in mouth, casually approach me.

"You volunteer?"

"Yes . . . are you from the baby orphanage?"

"Yes. Come with me."

I leave the airport terminal into the fumes of traffic and ultimately a Lada, the kind of car you probably drew when you were four years old: a box on top of four scooter-sized wheels surrounded by metal in the form of a car. The driver next takes me on a bumpy and roller-coaster drive through traffic, on tram rails (to avoid car traffic), over curbs (to cut corners), and finally into the dirt yard of a fenced-in compound.

It is a beautiful, two-story villa with crumbling yellow paint. Rusty playground equipment lies scattered in a yard overgrown with grass and weeds. A ten-foot impenetrable wall with barbed wire over the top surrounds the compound. What am I to expect? I have no idea; and neither does the staff awaiting me. From what I gather, they found out about my arrival only three days earlier and were told that a Down's syndrome specialist was coming. I am not such a specialist, I inform them. They tell me they are sorry that they have no bedroom, but would this old classroom suffice? After all, I have a couch to sleep on, a bathroom off to the side, and even a refrigerator in the entrance hall! I suddenly feel lucky that I have a place to stay. I am embarrassed that my arrival has put them out of sorts, and express my gratitude and apologize as they leave me to unpack.

The director, a slender, fashionably dressed, middle-aged woman leads me to her ornate office. There I am formally introduced to the staff in charge: the director, who is also the head pediatrician; a speech therapist, who prides herself on spending one hour a month with each of the sixty children in the three- to five-year-old groups; a nurse, who oversees most medical issues; and a pedagogue, who monitors educational activities in the groups. Each is exceptionally well dressed in high heels and office suits and dresses. I am surprised. Few Russians can afford such clothes.

Where are the orphans, I ask as I am wined and dined. Ah yes, a tour of the home is in order. I enter the room with the babies ages zero to nine months: swaddled in white cloth diapers, some with their arms exposed, others with their arms under the swaddle. Some cry. Why aren't they being held? They are crying! Response: We do not have enough staff to hold them, so they get held when they are fed. Do they always lie here? Yes. We do not have enough staff to take them out. We open the windows.

Next I am shown the room for one and two year olds. Half the room is fenced off for the toddlers to move about. The other half has high chairs. In the back bathroom, potties line the wall. Potties? At one? Yes, they learn early here. We do not have enough disposable diapers or the manpower to clean so many cloth diapers or time to put diapers on so many children, so we push them to learn as quickly as possible. As I make eye contact with the children, they reach out and start to cry. I pick up one. Immediately the child stops crying. The others are still crying, more heavily, noticing the unfairness of having not been picked. I put down the one in my arms and pick up another. The one I have put down sobs, the other one stops. "Don't pick them up too much," I am told. "They'll get used to it and when you leave, it will be more difficult for them."

I enter the room for three to five year olds. These are the children I will be working with. Upon entering I am immediately surrounded. Children ask to be held, to hold my hand; some pinch and pull my hair as I bend down. "For attention," I am told. I notice nice toys high on top of the shelves. "For decoration. Not to be played with," I am told. The children would, after all, only break these nice gifts from the West. The lower, more accessible shelves are almost bare.

As I am led back to my room I notice two doors that are locked. I am told that one leads to the Downs syndrome babies, who are currently quarantined due to the measles. I am not to visit these children until the quarantine has been lifted. "And the blue door on the other side of the room?" I ask. "It is better you do not enter that room. You do not want to see the children in that room. It's not necessary for your work and, well, you'll be better off if you do not go in." Better off. I wonder what that means. How could I be better off not knowing what is in the room next to the one in which I will sleep?

In the next six weeks, I would find out more than I anticipated about the care and upbringing of abandoned children in Russia. I will get to know even the most severely handicapped children as individuals who have emotions and personalities. I will see that each child has challenges, and that some even face death in the near future, but I will learn that each of these children is a unique person. Each of them will come to make a difference in my life. Soon I would find out what lay beyond the door and through it I will discover the meaning of abandonment and how suffering by the children and adults alike is seen as an inevitable evil. Throughout the summer, questions about these children will plague me, and eventually lead me to study abandoned children in Russia for the next decade and to write this book and try to answer some important questions: Why are these children neglected? What if they never receive tenderness? What kind of adults can they become? How can they ever be expected to be happy, healthy, productive citizens? My anthropological study will teach me to look deeper into the values and beliefs of Russians, which are a necessary aspect of understanding the answers to these questions.

PERSONAL BACKGROUND

My interest in Russia and abandoned children began in the late 1980s. I had decided that I wanted to study Russia from the perspective of an anthropologist, to learn about the Russians' world view, values, and beliefs from the inside out, from their point of view. I decided to use the concept of childhood as a lens into the Russian soul because in Russian society, as in many societies, parents, educators, and scholars emphasize the importance of childhood to the development of both the self and society. In both my personal and professional worlds, discussing childhood with family, peers, and colleagues had always engendered a deeper understanding of a person as a whole. In my New England college, students often explained who they were or why they thought and behaved in certain ways by prefacing their arguments with, "When I was growing up . . ." Such discussions helped me understand a friend's or colleague's motivations, beliefs, and values.

However, as I explored the world of childhood during my fieldwork in Russia in 1990 and 1991, I began to feel that something was missing. No one ever mentioned orphans. These included institutionalized children and the physically or emotionally challenged. I had passed a few orphanages on my long commutes to work but had never been invited to enter one. Seeing the orphanages but never hearing about them made me curious. Sometimes the only sign that children actually lived in orphanages were the small plaques on the doors indicating the number of the orphanage. In the city orphanages, play areas were frequently walled off from the public.

As I began my inquiry into institutionalized children's childhoods in Russia, I was faced with the problem of accessibility, as few Russians were willing to allow me into these parts of society. I was given addresses of orphanages but little more. Even within the institutions, administrators were rarely willing to open their doors. Luckily, a few caregivers I met welcomed me, and so began my journey into the soul of abandoned Russia.

My summer in the Moscow baby orphanage gave me a view into the life of Russia's institutionalized orphans. However, Russia has many kinds of orphans. Some never enter institutions and live on the streets. While not one person working with orphans suggested I study Russia's street children, their presence is felt at every railway station, every metro tunnel, and in the markets. Eventually, in 1999, I was able to study these children. I returned to Moscow to live there for three years, regularly visiting shelters and programs for street children. Immersion into this part of abandoned Moscow was much more difficult than living in the orphanage: I did not have a captive audience, forced to be with me because of the physical limits of an institution. These children came to me on their terms and with a complete lack of trust of adults in general. With the help of a shelter director, an art therapist, and a volunteer in a soup kitchen, I was able to get to know a few children and meet with them over time.

Abandoned—покинутый (*pokinutyi*)—literally means thrown by the wayside, deserted. I refer to the children in this book as abandoned, but in Chapter 3 I will elaborate on the concept, as it has many layers of meaning. I quickly learned how hardened abandoned people in Russia are forced to become. Abandonment is pervasive from birth through old age. People are abandoned by each other and abandon each other as mothers, fathers, husbands, wives; children abandon their families, citizens abandon their country, government officials abandon their duties; Russians abandon their soil, their space, their environment. And finally, Russians feel abandoned—by their fellow Russian citizens, by their families, and by their government.

And then there are the staggering numbers. The Russian Children's Fund estimated in 2001 that approximately 2.5 million children were living on Russia's urban streets and 250,000 were surviving in Moscow alone.[1] According to the Ministry of Education of the Russian Federation, there were 700,000 orphans recorded in Russia in 2000. This number does not include noninstitutionalized children who are abandoned, such as street children. According to Human Rights Watch, 113,000 children in Russia have been abandoned to the state each year since 1996. Up to 5 million Russian children are labeled at risk.[2]

Beyond the numbers, there are the facts. Overcrowding, poor hygiene, malnutrition, and abuse hinder children from integrating into society after institutionalization. Most abandoned children become seriously ill or delayed at some point and are at risk of premature death. The results of institutionalization include a higher incidence of behavioral, cognitive, and language problems than for children in the general population. Orphanage workers regularly reminded me that the death rate for disabled children is higher than those in "normal" boarding schools with paying parents.

Government boarding schools are different from those for which parents pay. These schools, *internaty*, in theory differ from orphanages in that children in *internaty* supposedly have a family they may return to on weekends and vacations. However, often orphans live in *internaty* as well, due to overcrowding of orphanages. Within the boarding schools and orphanages, children are grouped according to age and normalcy. In the baby orphanage I studied, the "normal" children, who often included children with learning problems, speech problems, or other minor challenges, were grouped by age. Other groups included the severely handicapped children, the Down's syndrome group and children with temporary infectious illnesses.

Of the ones who survive orphanages, few integrate well into society. Many turn to crime, including prostitution, to get by, or they numb themselves with alcohol and drugs. Approximately 15,000 children leave state orphanages every year. Within a few years of leaving, 5,000 will be unemployed, 6,000 will be homeless, 3,000 will have criminal records, and 1,500 will commit suicide.[3]

THE ANTHROPOLOGIST'S EYE

I was taught before I arrived in Russia that as a social scientist I was to be as objective as possible, not to let my feelings get in the way, and to try to understand the "other," in this case the children, as cultural beings. However, upon finding myself in Russia, in the midst of crying children, tears rolling down cheeks that demanded kissing, arms reaching out and demanding to be held, all the formal training I had received in graduate school temporarily seemed meaningless. Against the advice of the teachers at the orphanage, I had to reach back to the children and pick them up. As I learned about the children, I also felt compelled to understand the emotions that motivated the professionals working with the children. I needed to understand why some chose to stay in the business of caring for orphans while others were repelled from the job. One woman, a professor of pedagogy, made her perspective clear before I even embarked on my studies of orphans:

If you see a street child, it is better that you walk away. Don't try to talk to them. You cannot trust them and they do not trust you. It has always been like that and nothing has changed. They are damaged goods. Now, if you see a gypsy child, it is best you run away. Walk to the other side of the street or something. If you see one, there can be another thirty or so lurking, ready to surround you and take everything you have. They are sneaky. We all know that about gypsy children. You know, most of them aren't even poor, but rich! I was told by a friend that after a day of begging, they are picked up in Mercedes cars and driven home! Don't trust them![4]

The lives of abandoned children result from underlying cultural understandings of them. Traditional beliefs, subconscious though they may be, affect the lives of these children today. Even the most educated might have strong feelings about street children that are developed through hearsay, rather that knowledge of facts, as the quote demonstrates. When such views are passed on from generation to generation, they are rarely questioned and the stereotype is fixed.

Some beliefs that Russians will express and that affect how they view others and themselves include concepts of the soul and its connection to patience and suffering. While Russians agree that patience and suffering are woven through their history and culture, they disagree on how to react to the terms. Many Russians will take these terms to characterize their plight historically as victims. To many Russians whom I interviewed, orphans are similar to the average Russian in that they suffer. They are extreme victims, but mirrors nonetheless of the experiences of the peoples of Russia.

Others interviewed view suffering and victimization as signs of weakness, terms that need to be overcome. These Russians might feel the need to get ahead, often through business. It is thus no accident, as discussed in Chapter 2, that many know Russians as, on the one hand, soulful and, on the other, as materialistic. Extreme cultural terms demand extreme reactions.

Even with such diverging responses, the terms *soul, patience,* and *suffering* (and I would add *endurance*) are valuable to the ethnographer studying a particular culture. Terms, metaphors for larger meanings, symbols, and systems of communications, are the essence of culture and direct the outsider to what is important to the community being studied. Anthropologist Robert LeVine explains:

[E]very human community functions with a group consensus about the meanings of the symbols used in the communications that constitute their social life, however variable their behavior and attitudes in other respects, because such a consensus is as necessary for encoding and decoding messages in the social communication in general as agreement about speech rules is to encoding and decoding in the linguistic mode.[5]

Expressions in the form of language and communication are invaluable, no matter how great the differences are between individuals, in that they indicate the significance of the form of expression, the symbol that encapsulates a larger meaning.

While some anthropologists have tried to study culture as objectively as possible by focusing on social structure rather than on the individual self and emotions, I can only explain the life of orphans by talking about them as subjective beings. To understand any group of people, one must consider their emotions, reflections, personal expressions, and religious and mystical beliefs. I include subjective experiences to help the reader understand what it means to be abandoned in Russia. The lives of the marginalized (specifically, abandoned children) are furthermore relevant to understanding Russia as a whole. Stories about the marginalized, that is, about "what has been taken for granted, what has been neglected, regions of resistance, the forgotten, the irrational, the insignificant, the repressed, the borderline,"[6] tell us much about the greater society that has rejected them.

My argument, which sides with the belief in the importance of the mind, self, and emotion, is that Russian culture and tradition is all about experience, feelings, reflection, and expression, and it is precisely the emotion that must be examined in any analysis of Russia and her people. Yale Richmond, a prominent scholar, explains in his book *From Nyet to Da: Understanding the Russians,* "Human feelings count for much in Russia, and those who did not share the depth of these feelings—Americans among them—will be considered cold and distant."[7] In order to get close to Russians, to truly know them, one must be open and true to feelings. To understand Russia and Russia's abandoned children is to understand something intangible, something beyond structure and objectivity.

Studying a culture from an anthropologist's perspective not only gives insight into people, their behavior, ideologies, worldviews, and much more, but it also shines light on our own culture. By studying children and childhood in Russia, for example, I naturally thought about my own childhood, how Americans raise their children and to what extent childhood is valued and nurtured in the United States. By studying underprivileged children, we begin to think about those in our society. As we analyze the reasons for inequality in Russia, we learn more about what motivates inequality in the United States as well. As a result of addressing issues of poverty, inequality, and abandonment in Russia, we are better able to help the situation in Russia and also to bring back new ideas for our own society.

As Russia is evolving away from a socialist society, one of the fallouts has been the victimization of the weakest. Children all over the world suffer, yet the suffering in Russia has only recently been brought to the attention of the West. Certainly the tragic increase in numbers of homeless children is a new or, rather, renewed phenomenon since the collapse of the Soviet regime. It is the hope of the author that by catching the development of homelessness and child victimization at its earliest phase, the trend can be more readily mitigated and avoided in the future in countries facing similar social upheavals.

Child abandonment touches the hearts of most people. While it has been debated in scholarly writings exactly when childhood became accepted in the West as a special time in a person's life that is to be nurtured and understood,[8] most people today would agree that it is different from adulthood, that it is a special time of life, a time when we are filled with curiosity and potential. When children are born, we want the best for them, although it is not reflected in the salaries of educators or child caretakers. To the more philosophically minded, the demise of childhood signals the demise of civilization. "Children are the living messages we send to a time we will not see."[9] If we destroy childhood, we will self-destruct.

Understanding childhood as an esteemed time in a person's life, it seems preposterous that in only a few generations, children may not experience this time of life. That instead, childhood and adulthood may be one and the same thing: Children will be accepted as sexual beings, as workers, as criminals, as all the things we are as adults. Postman argues that indeed, childhood is disappearing "at dazzling speed."[10] He assumes that we care, and rightly so. Few would argue that if this is the case, that it is acceptable. Victimized children are seen as a tragedy and for this reason alone, abandonment must be resolved.

In Russia, the facts about abandoned children demonstrate the need for intervention and assistance. To some, they are frightening and demoralizing. Yet, this book takes statistics only as a springboard to tell a tale behind these facts that is even more daunting: Behind each number, there are real children, with real personalities and real stories to tell. In the baby orphanage, we will meet Galina, a victim of polio who spent her entire days in a crib in the "forbidden room" among children who could not speak or move. We will also learn about Pasha, a boy from St. Petersburg whose parents both died in an automobile accident and who refused to give up hope that his grandmother would one day come to take him home. We will learn about life on the streets through the eyes of Kolya, who had high hopes at the age of twelve of being adopted by an American family.

We will hear from the adults working with the children who also have a story to tell—how they found themselves working with the most rejected children in Russia and how they feel about their jobs. Mixed feelings of concern and resentment follow caretakers in orphanages through their days, making it difficult for them to respond tenderly to the children craving their love.

Motivating each story, there are a culture and traditions supporting a vicious cycle of poverty and neglect. The stories are about suffering and survival, about losses and accomplishments, about nightmares and dreams. This cultural background will also be discussed to illuminate the unique history and reasons behind child abandonment in Russia.

Chapter 1

Institutionalized, Neglected Orphans

What better time of life can there be than when the two finest virtues—innocent gaiety and a boundless yearning for affection—are the only mainsprings of one's life?

—Leo Tolstoy, *Childhood*, 1852

BACKGROUND

I have arrived at the orphanage in Moscow and am finally lying on my makeshift bed, a couch, in an old classroom, trying to sleep. I cannot. Three closed doors in the room stare out at me. One door leads to an exit, the others to orphans' rooms that I have been told not to enter. One of these rooms houses babies who have Downs syndrome; these children are under quarantine because they have the measles. The second room contains children from group number eight. The orphanage director forbade me from entering their room. The children, she said, are too "shocking."

It is past midnight. Howls and moans issue from the orphans' rooms, especially from the room housing group number eight. Finally, I can't stand it anymore. I get up and quietly I open the door to this room and enter. In the room's dim light I can see half a dozen cribs, some of them too small for the bodies they contain. I see children with heads twice the normal size, others with heads half the normal size, arms flailing, legs kicking. Children are whimpering and gasping, their eyes wide open without focusing.

I have to stop the noise. I have to comfort these beings. Inside an oversized crib in the center of the room, six children lie on their backs. They have not even noticed my presence. I go to the pen, and put one hand on one tummy, the other on another tummy, and whisper, "It's okay. Everything is okay." What am I saying? Nothing is okay. These kids are in serious need of help, of medicine, of therapy, of love. The thought makes me panic. How can I help these children at this time of night, with their caretaker away in another room watching television with her colleagues and drinking tea? I rub the children's tummies, and the two under my hands close their eyes. Success! They are sleeping! I go to the next crib, and the next, until I have touched every child. Not all of them respond, but all seem soothed, at least for a few minutes. Returning to my room in the early hours of the morning, I try to sleep. I cannot. Why are these children so neglected?

For the next month, I would live in baby orphanage number two, trying to help where help was needed and taking children aside to work on drawing and role-playing. The orphanage, in a suburb of Moscow, was home to infants and children up to six years old who had no family, as well as to children whose families could not take care of them and children with emotional or physical disabilities. During my stay at the orphanage and through research I conducted from 1990 to 2000, I found some answers—albeit not comforting ones—to the question that prevented me from sleeping that first night in the orphanage.

The emotional neglect of the orphans I worked with in Moscow is only one example of a problem that exists throughout Russia. Increasing numbers of children are being marginalized and discarded throughout Russia as the nation struggles to cope with its overwhelming economic and social problems. Since the 1991 coup that led to the dissolution of the Soviet Union, Russia has encountered an annual decline in population of .02 percent, with 31 percent of the population living below the poverty line and a decline of the gross domestic product of −4.6 percent.[1] This crisis has completely altered the face of Russia's rural and urban landscapes. Those who bear the brunt of these changes are those least equipped to cope with them, especially children.

Under the Soviet regime, children were hailed as the future of modern society and the responsibility of all adults. Since the end of Soviet communism, thousands of children have been labeled as *nishchie*, unwanted beggars. This label has been extended to include children in orphanages as well as other institutionalized children, disabled children, and children living on the streets and in gangs.

My stories are about the lives of children who, for various reasons, are confined behind the walls of a baby orphanage, a children's home, or an *internat*. Most helpful to understanding the environment in which the children are raised is the information collected from interviews with several caretakers who work in the orphanages. This environment is often, but not always, a hostile one in which the caretakers rarely show love and affection toward their charges. The caretakers themselves experience stress both in and outside work, which affects the young children whom they are supposed to nurture. Another factor contributing to the children's stress is the handling of children in institutions, which is done in a sterile way, with little love. However, throughout this journey through abandonment in Russia, we must remember that this is not new and that there are deep-rooted cultural underpinnings that have molded the way in which many Russians view abandoned children.

EXPANDING CULTURAL DEFINITIONS OF INSTITUTIONALIZED CHILDREN

My interest in Russian orphans began the year before my stay at the Moscow orphanage. I had originally set out to investigate the lives of Russian children and the attitudes of adults toward them in order to study issues such as socialization and education. My research led me to work in kindergartens, conduct interviews with teachers and parents, and take courses at the Gertzen Pedagogical University (at the time only an institute) on education and psychology. However, on my daily trips to the various schools and homes, I often found myself passing one particular building: an orphanage. While I felt welcome at most of the institutions I visited, my questions about the orphanage remained unanswered. It was not until the day I simply walked into the building with no invitation that my curiosity led me to include orphans in my project. It was here that I found contradictions between the dreams adults hold for their children and the reality many children in fact experience.

As a student of Russian language and literature, I was familiar with Leo Tolstoy's writings on childhood. In Tolstoy's view, the main focus of a child's life should be the family, whose members shelter children from adult worries and tribulations. Tolstoy, and certain other authors, helped create specifically Russian conceptions of childhood.[2]

In my interviews with Russian parents and teachers, I found that many Russians derive their conceptions of childhood from literature. In fact, many of the people I interviewed would express their views on childhood by quoting a well-known author such as Tolstoy. As one parent wrote on a questionnaire, "I want my child's life to be like the one described in Tolstoy's *Childhood*." Some Russians praise childhood as a carefree time of life and use Tolstoy's description of his own fictionalized childhood to represent their feelings about it.

However, during my visits to the homes and schools of children in St. Petersburg, and later during my stay in Moscow, I began to realize that one group of children never garnered the "gaiety" and "affection" of Tolstoy's idealized childhood. As I learned more about the lives of abandoned children in Russia, I was struck by the lack of attention and love these children received.

It was evident then, as it is now, that the Russian public views orphans as a threat. Rather than helpless victims, the children are seen as hopeless cases who threaten the well-being of society. Young orphans are placed in institutions and removed from daily social life until they reach school age. Orphans are then expected to attend regular schools, but many avoid doing so or attend schools in the orphanage. Of the adults I interviewed in 1990, only one recalled ever sitting in a classroom with an orphan.

The Tolstoyan ideal of childhood applies with certain restrictions. In my conversations with Russians, I have found that Russians generally believe that the ideal is practically unattainable for most children. Russians also believe that the purity and innocence are not automatically conferred upon every child. Those traits depend upon the purity of the child's parents. "Just look at the adults who abandon their children or who have them taken away!" One caretaker exclaimed. "How can the child be different? She has their blood."

Many Russians believe that orphans are inherently different from children who have homes. Neurologically, they are wired differently, according to the caretakers of one home, because they have not received the same love and attention that a "normal" child receives from his or her mother. Galya T., a teacher at the Moscow orphanage, explains: "These children are very different from children with homes. First of all, they have a different nervous development. They are more nervous. Children at home are calmer. Here, when one child cries, all cry. I don't remember that being the case at home. Their emotional state is different."[3] According to the same caretaker, orphans are sick, mentally and physically, and therefore attach quickly and indiscriminately, yet only superficially, to any newcomer. This is believed to be a result of the "unfortunate families" from which they come.

Today, Russians have mixed feelings about orphans. While little hope remains for them in their future, Russians do wish that they at least receive love. Caretakers especially pity the children they watch because they know firsthand the problems these children face from within and without. From within themselves, these children are unstable and come with a history of emotional baggage. From without the boundaries of their bodies, they are rejected. According to one caretaker interviewed, orphans are worthless.

This concept of the worthlessness of an orphan is one reason few Russians adopt children. When asked why adoption is not an option for some childless couples, the response was almost unanimous: "Because of the paperwork and because neighbors would 'talk.'" As one teacher told me, often a woman who cannot have a child will adopt one so that she does not become the talk of the town. A woman who cannot have a child is a reason for gossip and, behind her back, may be considered an incomplete woman. Once a couple has adopted a child, the family will often move to another city so that no one will find out that the child was an orphan.

The negative attitudes caretakers show toward orphans leads to an ironic self-fulfilling prophecy. Raised by caretakers who believe they are tainted and tell them they are worthless, institutionalized children develop a negative self-image. They are unable to envision a good future for themselves. This negative self-image may drive the orphan to crime and drug abuse, which, in turn, makes people mistrustful of him.

THE WORLD OF A RUSSIAN ORPHAN

Institutionalized children in Russia are commonly kept within the boundaries of the institutions. However, as they get older, orphans often end up roaming the streets. Within the orphanage, children share all material goods—toys, clothes, linens, and the like. Toys for older children are locked up and only brought out at certain times. Orphans rarely have their own toys, since these get stolen as soon as they are received. Some orphans hide their possessions or ask that a teacher hide a toy for them. One teacher showed me the small car given to her by an orphan in an orphanage. She told me how the child gave her the toy and comes to view it every now and then. The child is afraid to play with it because he is afraid that playing with the toy will create an opportunity for another child to steal the toy. The orphanages of the Soviet regime discouraged material possessions and fostered the notion of communal property and communalism in the name of scientific socialism.

During the day orphans attend schools either in the orphanage or outside the orphanage. In mainstream schools, orphans rarely make friends with the children who are not orphans and they are shunned by those children's families. Rarely are they invited to another child's home. Orphans have a harder time keeping up in school because they receive little to no help with their assignments, and only rarely do they go on to higher education. Most of the orphans who do continue with their education enter technical schools at the age of sixteen where they specialize in specific labor skills. Schools appear to orphans as hostile rather than nurturing environments, as institutions to be avoided rather than cherished. One orphan explained to me, "I do better for myself on the street."

The disdain for orphans in public areas is one reason for orphans' lack of success in society. This disdain is, however, so deep rooted that there is little hope for change in the near future. The disdain is accompanied by low expectations, discrimination, and alienation, all part of a larger understanding of orphans as genetically deficient, as having bad blood.

According to the caretakers in the Moscow orphanage where I resided and at other orphanages I visited, the best way to handle "bad blood" is to train an orphan as one might an animal; this method enables an orphan to cope with society. At the baby orphanages in Russia, children live a regimented life, with little room for creativity (except for their own games they come up with during free play) and no support for their emotional development. As one might train a robot to perform duties, these children are rarely held, touched, or cuddled.

By the age of eighteen months, the children are trained to use the potty and feed themselves with a spoon. By age two, they dress themselves. Voices are to remain low at all times inside and when children get hurt or upset, they are trained to comfort themselves.

At the baby orphanage in Moscow, the day begins at 6 o'clock in the morning, with a tired caretaker from the day before embarking on her last three hours of duty. Lyuba V. wakes the children up by opening the curtains and saying, "It's time to get up. Hurry, hurry!" She is very serious at this time since she has slept very little (if at all, for the caretakers are not allowed to sleep at night when they are on duty; they work twenty-four-hour shifts) and cannot wait to get off duty at 9:00 A.M. The children are given little time to wake up, with even less time to go to the bathroom, before they are scrubbed and told to eat their breakfast.

By 7:00 A.M., the children are ready for breakfast. But first, since Lyuba is working this morning, the children have to go out and do their morning exercises. The other teachers do not enforce this rule. Lyuba urges the children to line up in single file and marches them out into the courtyard. Here they walk in a circle while raising their arms, jogging, and jumping. Lyuba herself is a heavy woman and apparently out of shape, so the morning exercises do not last for more than fifteen minutes.

At 7:30 the children are back in the room playing, while Lyuba rushes to the kitchen to obtain the morning porridge. Upon her return, the children have to put away their toys, which they do quickly. At the table there is always some fussing about who gets what piece of bread, who put their bread into Aliosha's porridge, and the like. The teachers are very strict about silence at the table, and so the children are reprimanded. They all get one piece of bread with butter, sweet porridge (rice, oat, or wheat), and juice. The children face a day of overwhelmed and cynical caretakers—overwhelmed by and struggling to cope with the rapid social changes, cynical about the possibility of these children developing positively.

Most of the caretakers have chores outside their direct supervisory duties, and so most prefer to interact with the children as little as possible as a coping strategy to catch their breath before returning home to their own children. On top of dealing with this twenty times over for each of the children in their care, caretakers must struggle with making ends meet and caring for their own families while waiting in queues for food, struggling with rising prices, dealing with overcrowded public transportation, and suffering from various health problems due to affordable but poor medical facilities and a bad environment (contaminated water and air, general pollution, etc.).

By the time they come to work the caretakers are often short tempered and reproach children with phrases such as *"zakroi rotik"* (close your little mouth), *"tikho"* (quiet), and *"Ya tebia cherez zabor broshu!"* (I will throw you over the fence!). Children are rarely engaged in a conversation of more than a few words with the adults, adding to communication and language development issues. What children do learn from their adult caretakers is how to scold and scorn.

By 11:30 A.M., the children wash up for lunch. They sit around tables, either indoors or outdoors, depending on the weather. For lunch they eat soup, bread, meat patties, and boiled potatoes with slight variations during the week. Sometimes they get noodles instead of potatoes. Some children, like Vitalii, a pale-faced boy, thin, with dark, teary eyes and dark hair, eat slowly and have to be fed after a while. The caretaker will bend over the child and scoop in tablespoon after tablespoon at a fast pace. "That will teach him to eat faster next time," explains Tanya, one of the caretakers.

After an hour-long nap, the children go out to play, weather permitting. This is not the case for group number eight, the one in the forbidden room, the one with handicapped children. These children spend their time in beds. While "healthy" children face neglect and suffer developmentally, their physical health is guarded to the best of the caretakers' abilities. They are washed, given cold baths to promote health (a Russian tradition), taken outdoors as much as possible, and given medicine when available. Special needs children, however, while kept sufficiently clean and given medicine when available, are not taken into the fresh air or allowed to exercise. Like their healthy counterparts, they receive hardly any emotional or mental stimulation. Instead, they are left to lie or sit in the same room, day after day.

After the long play period during which caretakers relax, sit, and talk with one another, the children are ordered indoors and placed on potties. By the age of two, most orphans are potty trained and expected to go at specific times. After they wash their hands, dinner, similar to lunch, is rushed, after which a television period is sometimes added as a special treat. By 8:00 P.M. children are changed into their pajamas and told to go to bed. No good night kisses and hugs, simply lights out. The quicker they go to sleep the better, for now begins the physical work for the caretakers of cleaning the group rooms and getting ready for the morning. All this must be accomplished before 10 P.M., when the caretakers secretly convene in one room to have tea and watch their favorite program on television.

During my stay, I held and played with the children and treated the disabled as able. I developed a special relationship with a four-year-old girl named Galina. Galina, a delicate girl with a pale thin face and big brown eyes, was taken in by baby orphanage number two in Moscow because she had polio. From the day she entered in 1989 until I came in 1992, Galina had not been taken outdoors. As polio continued to rob her of her strength, she was no longer given the opportunity to sit upright, except for meals. She would be left in her bed all day and all night. Upon my arrival in the summer of 1992, I engaged her, took her outside (which made her laugh with joy), and worked with her on sounds. She learned words and learned to play.

The caretakers at the orphanage took offense to the attention I showed Galina and the other disabled children. They warned me that taking such children outside would only cause them to want more outside playtime, which the busy caretakers could not guarantee. I became a burden to them. "Don't play with her too much and don't hold her too much," one of Galina's caretakers told me. "She'll start missing you when you're not there and when you leave, she'll be even more upset than she is now. Don't spoil her."

These caretakers believed that disabled children are not as worthy as those who are "normal." They ranked children according to Russian beliefs of normalcy and gave each child the respective amounts of attention. The active, healthy children were allowed outside to play and even had special instruction from music and art teachers, while disabled children rarely went outside and almost never had special visitors from musicians or artists. The more handicapped, the more removed from the world they were kept.

Rather than nurture children physically and emotionally, the caretakers train the children to survive. When a child falls over and cries, she is told to get up quickly and to shut up. As one caretaker explains, "They have to realize that there won't be anyone there to pick them up in the future either. . . . Don't give these children too much affection. They'll always want more and will trample you to the ground. They will get out of control, so it's better to keep them at a distance." When a doctor at the orphanage momentarily breaks this rule by holding and comforting a child, she later regrets her actions. "After that," she says, "all my jewelry gets ripped, my hair is a mess, and they start to poke and pinch."

THE CARETAKER'S PERSPECTIVE

A number of problems exist in the orphanage system that are not unlike the problems orphanages in Russia faced in the nineteenth and early twentieth centuries: There are too many children and too few caretakers. As was the case historically, children in this overburdened system have learned to fend for themselves in a world that is often cruel and ruthless.

Caretakers have one goal in mind when handling young orphans: to prepare them for survival. By the age of one, children are well on their way to being potty trained, and by age two they are expected to feed themselves. Caretakers preach these survival skills to prepare children for their life in the *detskii dom*, the orphanage for older children. No one will look after their nutritional intake and feeding oneself is an important tool. One caretaker explains, "If they don't learn to eat, they will die when they enter the next orphanage. There, nobody supervises what the children eat or how much, and they certainly don't have time to feed them there."[4] Once again, children are compared to stray animals that need to get by, scavenging and fighting for survival.

Caretakers at orphanages often feel embarrassed about their jobs. Teaching is not a respected career in Russia. If a teacher works with the lowest common denominator of students (i.e., orphans), then she is very likely to lack motivation in her job. Moreover, many of the caretakers I spoke with in a baby orphanage in Moscow felt that they had come to the position not by choice. One caretaker, Tanya, had come to Moscow to become a singer. Unfortunately, her own family life did not make her dream possible.

My childhood wasn't bad, except for the fact that my father drank a lot. When he drank, he wouldn't come home, slept everywhere . . . and we were usually brought to other homes, family members, neighbors, and so on. I was his favorite. He didn't like my brother as much. Whenever I was in trouble, I would hide behind him and if he wasn't home, I'd go somewhere else until he came home. I did play a lot with my brother. We always had clothes and food. Both my parents worked. We lived outside the city. My mother took care of fifty cows. I don't know what's better, the city or the country. You see, I sang quite well and had I been in the city, I would have become a singer. But instead, I clean potties.[5]

At this, Tanya sighs. She feels debased in her job at the orphanage.

A pediatrician in the same orphanage, Nina M., reacts similarly. She resents her current position:

I wanted to be a biologist. I love flowers and I used to show flowers I had grown. But I also like to help others. So I chose to study medicine, but I didn't get good grades and so they sent me to the department of pediatrics. That's where you go when the university does not think you'll be a good doctor.

As I discovered by talking to Nina M., not only is working with orphans debasing, but being a children's doctor is seen as inferior to treating adults.[6]

Because orphans are marginalized in Russian society, so are their caretakers. As a result, caretakers feel humiliated and tainted by their association with the children. Orphanage workers do not tell others where they work if they can avoid doing so. Instead, some choose to live a clandestine life and come to work on a daily basis with negative feelings toward their jobs and the children.

The negative feelings of the teachers carry over to the general morale at the orphanage in Moscow. Tanya M., a small five-year-old girl with short blond hair and large blue eyes, came to the orphanage after being found near a dumpster as an infant. She was always on the lookout for her mother and always hopeful when a stranger visited. She once told me, "My teacher is not my mama. She is always angry with me. My real mama is coming to get me soon. She loves me."[7] Caretakers not only insult, offend, and humiliate the children, but moreover, they also treat them as invisible, as somehow nonhuman. Children are rarely held (in contrast to children in the traditional Russian family, who are coddled by all members of the family). According to the caretakers, there are not enough adults to hold the children, so none get held. As a result of this unloving environment, the children are stressed and unhappy. Their feelings are expressed both physically and in their behavior. Physically, the children suffer skin and bowel disorders. Behaviorally, temper tantrums that last up to an hour are the norm. Fighting between the children is broken up without a word spoken between caretaker and child, except for the scolding that may ensue.

When caretakers in the baby orphanage claim that their goal is not to coddle the children but to train them for life, in a sense they know what they are saying. Life for older children in an orphanage is about survival of the fittest. Once in the *detskii dom* (orphanage for children seven and older), the new and weaker will inevitably be tested by the older, more experienced. In a Human Rights Watch report, this testing or *dyedovshchina* was compared to hazing in U.S. college fraternities, albeit a much crueler and more violent version. Not only do older orphans seek to keep their high ranking position and control over others, but also the caretakers will use older orphans to punish others or even for pure entertainment.[8]

Some of the punishments are so common that they bear names. As collected by Human Rights Watch, here are some examples:

Makaronina (little macaroni): The child rocks his head to the left and right. While doing that, someone strikes each side of his neck.

Fashka (no real translation): The child fills his cheeks with air and someone hits him on the cheek. It is very painful because his teeth cut the inside of his cheek.

Locya (deer): The child has to stand with his palms crossed, facing out, on his forehead. Someone beats the palms with his fist so that the knuckles hit the child's forehead. It is very painful.

Oduvanchik (dandelion): An older kid beats with fists on top of the head of a younger child.

Velociped ("bicycle"; well known in the army): When someone is in bed, balls of cotton are put between his toes. The cotton balls are set on fire and the person kicks his legs as if he is peddling a bicycle.[9]

This type of social control by orphans of orphans, resulting in ranking, hazing, and dominating, is a historical phenomenon in Russia. In the nineteenth- and early twentieth-century Russian orphanages, rule by orphans frequently outweighed adult control.

The practice of punishment by older orphans, however, does not preclude punishment by adult staff members. According to children's accounts, examples of punishment include putting the child's head in a toilet, beating, withdrawing food, verbal and public humiliation, twisting of body parts, and isolation in cold rooms. The following are quotes from some of the Human Rights Watch report's documented abuses:

In one case:

The teacher would punish children by bringing everyone into the classroom, and then making the ones who did something wrong get undressed and stand in front of the open window when it was very cold. Several children would be stripped and have to stand like that while the others had to watch the child in front of the window as a threat.

In another case:

For punishment, a teacher . . . would strip off a child's clothes until he was completely nude and make him get down on all fours. Then the rest of the children had to kick the child and sit on him like a horse to humiliate him. The kids could push and kick and pull hair and ride him like an animal. She was an active sadist.[10]

Human Rights Watch found consistency in testimonies of children across Russia, confirming widespread corporal and verbal abusive punishment of children in orphanages by the caretakers.

THE OLDER INSTITUTIONALIZED ORPHAN

Lacking in emotional, physical, and intellectual development, and not having been exposed to the concepts of love and security, the six-year-old orphan leaves her baby orphanage and enters the *detskii dom*, the children's orphanage and public school. At the *detskii dom*, the child is thrown into a system that has two sets of rules: that of the caretakers and that of the orphans who live there. The rules of the older orphans outrank those of the caretakers and involve traditions similar to but worse than fraternity initiations: Beatings are common and no child can own anything. The rooms are bleak, containing the bare minimum: beds, sheets, a dresser with a lamp, a few chairs, and desks.

Upon entering one such room at an *internat* outside the city of St. Petersburg, I was engulfed by a smell of smoke. In response to my question as to the root of the smell, Pasha, a ten-year-old orphan, pointed his finger at a black, smoldering spot in the middle of the room. "We built a fire. We were pretending to camp!" To my astonishment, no caretaker seemed concerned.

On another occasion at the same *internat*, Pasha gave me a tour of the sleeping quarters of the younger children. There, children ages six and seven shared rooms in groups of ten. When I came by, it was the end of naptime. I entered the group room only to find the temporary group teacher, no older than sixteen, making out with her boyfriend. Upon seeing me, she jumped to her feet, wiped her mouth, and told me to please come in. She opened the door to the children's sleeping quarters. Here I was met by terrified children who jumped on their beds as I entered. The leader of the group, a pail, thin, wild-eyed girl yelled, "Who are you? A foreigner? A Nazi?" It was not until I handed out some candy that the children calmed down. Once comfortable with my presence, they clung to me and hugged my legs or any limb they could grab. At one point I had one child per finger, holding on desperately, as if life depended on it. I later found out that they were not used to outsiders, much less foreigners, coming to visit and that I was perhaps the first American they had ever seen. At this *internat*, outside of class, children took care of children. The orphans were left to fend for themselves, and at times they became wild. Here the children appeared territorial, aggressive, rank conscious, hungry for attention, skeptical, and afraid of adults.

The life of an orphan is one of uncertainty, irregularity, and hostility. From the baby orphanage that surrounded the child with ambivalence to the *detskii dom* of fending for themselves, the children's lives are based on survival of the fittest. By the time a child is eight, frustration is evident in the child's drawings. One sees anger in the pressure they put on the crayon, their choice of colors (dark or bleak), and their choice of subjects—weapons of various kinds, death, blood. Violence becomes a part of their daily lives, as they defend and protect all they have left: their bodies.

At school, orphans are ignored and shunned by peers. They cannot keep up academically and do not know the rules of the average child's world. They may respond inappropriately to social circumstances and often lash out violently toward their peers. Some orphans run away. In play, an orphan is a serious warrior, not a playmate, and will be quick to use his or her fists if losing is in sight.

Most institutionalized children take to the streets to earn a living as soon as they can, sometimes by the age of seven, rather than going through traditional social means of education first, then work. However, as orphans, they endure second-class status throughout their lives.

Special needs children in Russia generally do not have the option of going to school. Instead, they are deemed uneducable and are placed in psychoneurological boarding homes for children. If these children show any signs of violence toward others or themselves, they are not offered psychological counseling. Instead, they are restrained by being tied to furniture, placed in cloth sacks, or other methods. When they reach adulthood (if they survive these boarding homes), they enter regular psychological institutions. According to Human Rights Watch, such institutionalized adults are denied their civil and political rights.[11]

It is clear that the social taboos against abandoned children and the resulting lack of social help they receive leads to a dismal future adulthood for these orphans. Not until Russians can visualize the potential of the orphans as functional members of and participants in adult society will any progress be made. The taboo against orphans runs too deep and is too widespread for orphans to succeed and live happy and productive lives. Despite some caretakers who behave differently by treating orphans with love and respect, overall the outlook for orphans is bleak. Most orphans experience the repercussions of their damaged childhoods during their adult lives, as they struggle to find housing, food, and jobs.

Chapter 2

Victims of a Failed System, or Cold Cultural Beliefs?

You ask me what I want for my child? The perfect childhood! We all want that for our children. It should be a time when you are without concern or pain. I want my child to feel happiness. He should know rules, but these rules should not be too many or too complex. The more difficult problems must be taken care of by adults. I want my child's childhood to seem magical, like in a happy fairy tale. It is my job to see to it that my child is well fed, well clothed and content. That he feels that every day is a celebration.

—Olga T., 2002

ALL CHILDREN AS RUSSIA'S FUTURE?

As I walk through the parks and playgrounds in Moscow in the winter of 1999, I see signs everywhere of Russians' love for their children. Grandparents and parents follow their young in play, cuddling them when they can, making sure they are warm and protected. One grandmother beckons a child to come down the slide quickly, catches her and puts her on her feet, and reties the woolen hat and rebuttons the coat to make sure no unnecessary skin is subjected to the cold. While fresh air is necessary for good health, to these Russian grandmothers and mothers, being cold is detrimental, very possibly causing the flu. Babies are seen bundled in their carriages with their noses barely peeking out. One grandmother sits on a bench in the cold, rocking the carriage gently, clicking her tongue, and speaking gently, "There, there, enjoy the fresh air. Don't cry."

During the mandatory walk in the park for fresh air, grandmothers and mothers hover over their little ones, engaging them by speaking in a high voice, cooing, and delighting in every move their child makes. The grandmothers in particular appear to have given themselves completely to the raising of the young while the parents are at work. They barely have time to acknowledge a friend as they rush home to cook a warm meal for lunch, which must include a soup and a main dish with meat and vegetables. For the traditional Russian family, the children's well-being is the focal point.

A Russian childhood is not merely a stage of life defined in psychological terms. Rather, it is a socially constructed concept on which much historical weight is placed and that is connected to cultural notions of the past and the future of Russia. It is a concept intimately connected with nostalgia for the "ideal childhood," as it has emerged, deeply influenced by Russia's great thinkers such as nineteenth-century writer Leo Tolstoy. The ideal childhood as depicted by Tolstoy is one many Russian families wish to give their children, especially since many adults feel they were robbed of theirs due to harsh social circumstances. This personal loss of childhood has been described to me as connected to the Russian people's loss of their national childhood under the Soviet regime. Those who have survived and even thrived under the changes from Sovietization to democratization have hope that they can at least give their children the care and freedoms they lacked in their own childhoods.

As I leave the parks and head underground into the metro, I am confused. Unlike the children I just saw in the parks, here dirty, poorly clad, cold, and undernourished children sleep on cardboard. Some are begging or getting high. One boy rummages through the trash, unwrapping a bag and licking the remains of someone's shashlik (grilled meat on a stick). Dirt covers his face and hands, and sticky remnants of the glue he had been sniffing coats his nose. In one of the long underground tunnels, I find a woman sitting in the cold, holding an infant.

She is right in the center of the draft, and the blistering wind whips around her. Again, I am struck by the contrast of this child in the underground to the children bundled in their carriages in the park. Traditionally, a Russian grandmother would never allow herself and especially her child to sit on a cold floor in the draft. According to traditional belief, a draft will get you sick and a woman who sits on a bare floor will no longer be able to have children. When I first came to Russia in 1989, homeless children were rarely seen. However, since the collapse of the Soviet regime, they have become a common sight in large cities.

At first, this new phenomenon did not make sense. How could a society so geared toward the well-being of its children allow so many of them to suffer? My Russian colleagues argue that these children are simply the victims of a failed Soviet education system and of recent social changes. But I have found that the story of abandoned children is more complex. While social and educational problems certainly have enabled the number of abandoned children on the urban streets to climb, I have found that cultural beliefs dating back at least to tsarist times have also contributed to homelessness.

While many countries experience homelessness, not all of them have the same reasons for their homeless children. For some countries, economic circumstances are mainly to blame. For others, war or HIV infection is the primary cause. In Russia, cultural attitudes, how people subconsciously feel about and ultimately react to homelessness, fueled by historical circumstances, are equally important to understanding the plight of orphans and street children.

RAISING RUSSIA

At a time when youth gangs and street children seemed to be damaging the image Soviets wished to portray of an orderly society, where all the citizens' needs were met, Anton Makarenko was employed to reeducate juvenile delinquents into socially acceptable members of society. Makarenko, an educator, was assigned in 1920 to manage a children's home (later named the Gorky Colony) for "troubled youth," which included orphans and children with behavioral issues. Makarenko developed a philosophy on social education that combined education and upbringing. He criticized traditional schools and homes. According to him, school administrators were overly concerned with the economic welfare of the school and teachers were too busy teaching facts, while parents were not helpful either. He advocated a collective upbringing of children, one in which children learned from life with the support of the community and the family:

Each father and each mother must be well aware of what traits they wish to foster in their child. It is imperative to have a clear idea of one's own wishes as a parent. Ask yourselves if you wish to bring up a true citizen of the Land of Soviets who is well informed, energetic, honest, devoted to his people and the revolution, hardworking, optimistic and well mannered. Or do you want your child to turn into a greedy philistine, a cowardly, crafty, little go-getter? . . . And in all this, you should always remember: you gave birth and are bringing up your son or daughter not only for your parental happiness. In your family and under your guidance, a future citizen, activist and fighter is growing up. If you make a mistake and bring up your child badly, then the trouble will not only be yours but also that of many other people and the country as a whole. Do not brush aside this problem, considering it tedious philosophizing. Surely you are ashamed when your factory or institution turns out defective products. You should be even more ashamed if you present society with bad or harmful people.[1]

Socialists believed that the family would be one of the last traditional institutions erased when the ideal socialistic society was realized. Until then, the family would merely aid in the protection of children's interests.[2] Underlying this ideal was the assumption that the family impeded the realization of the ideal Soviet citizen and was the cause of problems with youth such as juvenile delinquency.

To change juvenile delinquents into respectable Soviet citizens, Makarenko took a rather military approach. His students were acknowledged only as parts of a collective, not as individuals. They were put to work and educated in the process of labor. Makarenko believed that the children were only as problematic as their environment and that a structured, strict, and disciplined educational environment, one that challenged the youth mentally and physically and forced them to work as a team, would yield a better person. He thus came up with the concept of a Children's Labor Army, an organization that would unify all institutions involved in the education and upbringing of children with a common ideological and pedagogical base. This unity would lead to all children, abandoned or not, attending one public education system based on the same ideas and philosophy, the goal of which would be to mold the individual, altering his character if need be, into a "loyal and worthy member of his collective, a citizen of the Soviet state."[3] To Makarenko, the ultimate goal in the upbringing of children was to create an ideal Soviet citizen.

However, even in Makarenko's day many pedagogues and parents criticized his system's lack of love and soul. While the Soviets did not support spirituality and the practice of religion, Soviet citizens continued to embrace a deep-rooted belief: the concept of the Russian soul. To this day, anyone studying Russia has heard it before: Russia has a soul and in Russia you can find true faith. The concept of the soul is deeply related to Russian history and the traditions of the past, making today's Russian soul all the greater. Russians are passionate in describing the concept of soul, and yet it is not something you can define in a word. Indeed, entire essays have been written on the subject.

To understand Russians and their views on raising children, one must understand, or at least appreciate, the meaningfulness of Russian soul, or *dusha*. Some scholars have tried to capture the essence of what is Russian soul. The most revealing analysis I have found is Pesmen's *Russia and Soul: An Exploration*.[4] This ethnography discusses the difficulty and even impossibility in pinning down soul, intangible as it is. At the same time, *dusha* is depicted as essential to understanding Russia. Soul is part of Russian everyday life. It is inherent in high culture, philosophy, and literature. It is sometimes used to describe Russian national character. In the past, Russian nationalists described their own national character as highly emotional and impossible to pin down or define. Russians to this day are known for being spontaneous, unpredictable, and even barbarian.[5] All of this can only truly be captured in one concept: *dusha*, or Russian soul.

In and of itself, soul evokes concepts of compassion and suffering, which in the 1990s was commonly "invoked in contexts of resistance to modernity, materialism, and hierarchy."[6] Soul is neither definite nor dispensable. Pesmen goes on to point out that it "reveals itself most often (though not only) when people are in extreme positions."[7] Russian soul is itself a broad concept incorporating the complexities of the Russian people. For that reason, soul may be investigated as a means to understanding the heart of Russian culture.

Most generally, part of the concept of Russian soul can be explained as follows: an indescribable "inner world," an expansive, authentic "life force," and essences of people, places, groups, and other things. Soul and dusha both often relate to compassion and suffering and are invoked in contexts of resistance to modernity, materialism, and hierarchy.[8]

While *dusha* may be compared to the Western notion of soul, it is also different. One way it differs is that *dusha* is an essential part of raising children. If children are raised without *dusha* and do not learn its meaning, Russians believe, they will have lost the essence of being Russian. Olga T., a mother and editor, tells me:

Orphans, they are empty. If they are lucky, they go to school and get educated. But that doesn't mean they understand themselves or what's important. They need soul, and that only their mothers can give them.[9]

Soul cannot be infused by any institution like a school or orphanage and yet it is an essential component to a Russian upbringing.

In Russian, the word "upbringing" (Воспитание) is used to describe a most important aspect of childhood. It is considered as equal to, if not more important than, the education a child receives in school. The importance of upbringing is described by Irina S., a teacher:

"Children are our future!" Of course, you already know this teaching of the Soviet regime. We still believe in that phrase. Surely you have read all the literature on Soviet pedagogy. From Lenin's wife Krupskaya, to the pedagogue Makarenko, all felt the need to develop a strong education system which will help the family raise future Soviet citizens. In fact, some of the pedagogues of the past viewed the family as a hindrance to the creation of an ideal Soviet person. But today, we feel that the upbringing depends on the parents. The schools certainly don't teach your children the things that are important, like about morality. And they certainly do not teach a child what it means to be Russian, to be proud, to understand the Russian soul or the suffering of the Russian people. In schools they only learn about past facts and how to get by and hopefully succeed. And to succeed these days, you can't depend on morality.[10]

Irina S. sums up history in few but succinct words. While Makarenko's ideas showed how to train juvenile delinquents and orphans to act appropriately in the Soviet collective, his pedagogy stripped the child of Russian soul.

However, today, within the ragged orphans that roam the streets, we can see that the Russian concept of soul has persisted. Russia's homeless children are the victims of social strife and symbolize the extremes and struggles Russian individuals experience on a daily basis. While Russian society recoils from and rejects these children, it also recognizes them as symbols of Russia's inherent tribulations.

These children are living the exact opposite of what we want for our children. On the one hand, we want to pretend they do not exist. It's an embarrassment to our country. Is not homelessness and begging to this degree a sign of a developing third world country? Stray dogs and street children in gangs: they represent extreme poverty and the inability of a nation to take care of itself. And yet, we cannot totally reject them. They represent an extreme and in doing so, they are a part of us. After all, is Russia not known to be a country of extremes? These children are the opposite of what we envision children in Russia to be like! They are without a home, without love and yet they are part of our country's soul.[11]

The notion, developed at the time Makarenko wrote, that some children are an embarrassment to the family or fatherland is one that continues to pervade Russian attitudes.

CHOSEN TO SUFFER

Some commentators describe contemporary Russia as the opposite of the soulful image history has portrayed. Instead, they say Russians are superficial and materialistic. You may hear that Russians have lost their faith, that they have lost any sense of their past and are now looking only to the West for guidance.

Both historically and today, both sets of assumptions are correct. George F. Kennan, a diplomat and historian who was known for his insights on Russian culture during the Cold War, noted in his memoirs:

Contradiction is . . . the essence of Russia. West and East, Pacific and Atlantic, Arctic and tropics, extreme cold and extreme heat, prolonged sloth and sudden feats of energy, exaggerated cruelty and exaggerated kindness, ostentatious wealth and dismal squalor, violent xenophobia and uncontrollable yearning for contact with the foreign world, vast power and the most abject slavery, simultaneous love and hate for the same objects. . . . The Russian does not reject these contradictions. He has learned to live with them, and in them. To him, they are the spice of life.[12]

Contradictions and extremes mark Russian history, culture, and society. To the Western observer, contradictory descriptions of Russians are unsettling. Yet because Russians accept these contradictions as part of the Russian way of life, the American researcher needs to come to terms with them. The Russian worldview may be best described by Fyodor Tyutchev in his famous poem "Umom Rossiu":

> Russia cannot be understood by the mind.
> She is not measured by a common ruler.
> She stands as unique—
> In Russia one can only have faith.[13]

In this poem, Tyutchev captures the spirit of Russia, which is, quite briefly stated, indefinable. Russia can best be captured in a poem because, unlike prose, poetry expresses emotion most efficiently and totally.

On the one hand, Russians are soulful, spiritual, and aware of the impact of their history on their lives today. On the other hand, Russians are tired of living in squalor and are trying to beat the system to earn a living and acquire basic comforts taken for granted in the West. Russia is a culture of extremes.

I have come to find that few Russians agree on any one description of Russia. However, there are two emotions that bind Russians:

terpenie (patience) and *stradanie* (suffering). I consider them essential to understanding any part of Russian culture and society. Patience and suffering are deeply imbedded in the Russian experience. The two are connected; Russians believe that the patience required of them goes hand in hand with the suffering they must endure. Russians themselves characterize their entire social history with these two terms and will argue that the Russian people have endured, rather than simply lived, their past.

There are Russian scholars and writers who have reflected on the importance of suffering and patience to the Russian psyche. Dostoevsky himself maintained:

I think that the most basic, most rudimentary spiritual need of the Russian people is the need for suffering, ever-present and unquenchable, everywhere and in everything. It seems that the *narod* [the population][14] has been infected with this thirst for suffering since the beginning of time. This stream of suffering runs through all its history, not only summoned by external misfortune and poverty, but welling up like a spring from the very heart of the people.[15]

In her book on Russian conversations recorded during perestroika, Nancy Ries argues that suffering characterizes the litanies heard in daily conversations, in which Russians agree about their plight. Litanies are also forms of communication that may effect "paradoxical value transformations," or moments in which certain states of being, like suffering, would add status to the speaker. For example, Ries shows how suffering distinguished one person from another who did not suffer or how having sacrificed in ones life gave that person a superior status.[16] Suffering is seen as a fact of Russian life, without which a Russian is not as honorable or truly Russian. To distinguish oneself both as a Russian and among Russians, one must suffer in Russia. One must endure.

In my journeys through Russia, I heard Russians describe patience and suffering. Under Gorbachev, life in Russia at times seemed burdensome: It was hard to come by anything basic. Luxuries such as chocolate seemed a figment of the past. Standing in lines to buy food, for example, one could hear grandmothers sigh, *"nado terpet' "* (one must be patient).

Because suffering is such a fundamental part of the Russian mentality, Russians can, to some degree, identify with the homeless. However, because others' suffering is also seen as almost a natural outcome of living in Russia, empathy is limited. Anyone who suffered more than most was viewed with pity but also with a certain ambivalence. Passing by a beggar, Russians were quick to comment, "We all suffer" or "It's hard for everyone." Suffering in Russia builds a sense of identity, a sense that we Russians are all in the same boat, that we Russians are all alike.

Upon passing homeless children, my friend Olga T. commented, "It's awful. I cannot look them in the eye. How can I help? I can barely help myself and my son. We are all struggling. To suffer and struggle is Russian." Indeed, the patience and suffering experienced by the homeless are Russian terms with which Russians identify, and in so doing, they identify with the homeless.

CHOSEN AS VICTIMS

Russians feel, and I would add rightly so, that they have traditionally been victimized by those in power. From before the tsars and throughout the Soviet regime, the general population lived in poor conditions, with hardly a voice, few rights, and few privileges. To lament their plight is part of Russians' daily communication.[17] Laments or "litanies" come in various forms, but most generally include complaining, grieving, or expressing worry. When standing in line at a store or at a bus stop, Russians will discuss their life problems quite freely and in a ritualized manner. The litany involves an entire ritual, beginning with a statement about afflictions, tribulations, or losses, sometimes even a list of these, and frequently ending in a poignant rhetorical question like, "Why is everything so bad with us?"[18] One particularly popular theme of the litany expresses the victimization of Russians throughout history by those in power and, ultimately, a feeling of doubt among Russians that their lives will ever be better. Victimization and suffering are part of the Russian soul. Many Russians agree that being Russian means being special because God has chosen Russia to suffer. As one acquaintance at a party once pointed out to me, "We are God's bad experiment. God has chosen us to demonstrate to the rest of the world how not to live."

Even Russian children express litanies. Children, with or without homes, may be heard blaming others (their families, the West, or fate, for example) for the hopelessness of their lives. While I heard many a homeless child lament her inability to move beyond poverty without taking a criminal turn, children who have homes also lament the plight of their Russian lives. In an interview with a seven-year-old girl we can see the litany already developing. Dressed in her neatly ironed school uniform, rocking in her chair, and rolling her eyes at the thought of her country, she insists:

I will live in another country. I cannot live here. . . . I have had enough. I'll have to marry someone from France. From Paris . . . I don't love this country. . . . Everyone screams "Perestroika! Perestroika!" What is the point of it? Goodness! Politics, they call it. They could at least give us something to eat! Caviar for instance.[19]

By the age of seven and even younger, children in Russia quite naturally lament their condition and the hardships of living in Russia, imitating the statements and gestures of adults they have witnessed over their life span.

Through its repetition and incantation, the litany expresses at once a common identity Russians feel. First, the litany establishes a connection to others who suffer as well. Indeed, one might call this a community of sufferers.[20] The recitation of the litany helps define a Russians' identity on various levels, including collective and national, and the relations between these levels.[21] In so doing, a speaker not only identifies herself with a group, but also alludes to her community's virtual superiority, by having suffered the most:

[L]itanies were thus always competitive, for to establish that your group was the most victimized of all was to achieve a specific kind of social virtue: the virtue of powerlessness in a context in which power was characterized as immoral or evil.[22]

While groups of Russians, such as veterans and minority groups, see themselves as more persecuted than others, Russians view themselves as basically similar because of their mutual suffering and endurance. To mention someone who may have suffered more or worse, is to undermine the average Russian's plight. As a result, Russians interviewed for this book tended to see the abandoned as similar to themselves on the level of suffering, yet as different in terms of moral background and upbringing. An orphan worker reminded me, "How good can an orphan really be? Look at where they come from and who their parents are. They will be the same because they will take after their parents."[23] Rather than acknowledge abandoned children as one of the most victimized communities in Russia, many Russians view abandoned children as different, unlike the average "we."

One of the greatest causes of their suffering, according to my Russian informants, are authority figures. Ironically, few Russians challenge authority. This submission to authority begins at the school level where, under Soviet rule, rote replies rather than individual responses were demanded. An emphasis on a right response that is memorized has its roots in the Soviet belief that the role of the school reaches beyond teaching subjects and extends to include the moral upbringing of children. As a result, scholars have noted that children educated under the Soviet system, "while usually ahead of American students in knowledge of their subjects, are much less likely to be able to think for themselves, and to have their own opinions."[24] When asked to give their own opinion, Russian children and adults alike might feel more comfortable quoting a famous author or politician than coming up with their own words.

Children are raised to fear authority figures from the very start. In school, children are given themes of what to draw and methods of how to draw. During my fieldwork in Russia, I encountered numerous occasions when children were even scolded for trying to be creative. From my field notes:

Now it is time to prepare for the afternoon art class. According to the program, this time is to be spent learning how to produce art and independent work. These activities are meant to stimulate an interest in art in the child and to strengthen drawing, clay-work, and collage skills. They also widen the child's perception of form, color, and structure, and develop emotional responses to art.

As class begins, the children sit at round tables, facing the teacher who has pinned a piece of paper to an easel. With a paint brush in one hand pointing at the paper, the teacher announces, "Today we are going to learn how to draw flags. We are going to draw three of them, in a line, across the page." The children are staring expressionless at the teacher. The teacher turns to the board and slowly demonstrates how the lines are to be drawn and adds, "If you like, you can draw and color them with different colors."

The demonstration is now over and the children dip their brushes into paint. Each table has at least three paint flasks, many of which are old and have been mixed with other colors. Some of the faster workers are done in five minutes. Among them are Lena and Zhenya. Lena is a very hard worker who usually completes her task quickly and outstandingly. Today she has decided to add something to her blank paper with only three flags on it.

At this age, when children are developing a sense of proportion, they often prefer to fill up blank spots in pages, to make their paintings seem even. Psychologists often can discover much about the development of the child by studying paintings and analyzing the configuration of lines and strokes on a page. Thus it would appear natural for Lena, an intelligent and creative child, to try and fill up her page and make it more aesthetically pleasing.

Lena decides to do so by painting balloons around the flag. Some of her balloons are spotted, others are colored, just like her flags. With a broad smile she looks up at me and I nod and smile approvingly. The teacher has noticed the disruption at our table and comes over. "What is all the fuss? You know you are to be quiet while painting. Lena, are you done?" Lena holds out her painting and encourages the teacher to look. "Look what I did!" The teacher takes one glance at the painting and starts, "What have you done! Don't you know that you were to paint only three flags? Once and for all, I have no need for your fantasy!" Lena becomes very quiet and looks away from me. I feel as if I have made a mistake by approving. I secretly tell her that I still like her paintings.

Russian children learn to endure authority at an early age. Homeless children are among the few in Russia who have challenged authority. During perestroika, when the social infrastructure began to crumble, the police focused less on maintaining an image of Soviet perfection on the streets. Children from broken or less-than-stable homes began taking to the streets. Moreover, with the loosening of social control, orphanage caretakers found it increasingly difficult to keep orphans inside the walls of institutions. Today, street children

pride themselves on having escaped the bondage of institutionalization and consider themselves lucky to be free.

Street children view the authoritarian rule within the orphanages
as equivalent to imprisonment and thus, any adult authority is seen as
a threat to their freedom and ultimate happiness. For example, in one
shelter in Moscow, the director told me how frequently certain children come to the shelter to get rest, food, and warmth, and then leave
as soon as they feel ready. No matter how hard he tries to persuade
them to stay, to go to school, and to accept the shelter as a home,
the children leave, reminding him that living outside the confines of
any institution, freely, that is, is better than living within. Homeless
children are, unknowingly, rebelling against their people's legacy of
enduring authority, and, in a sense, are pioneers in a developing Russian society.

CONCLUSION

Understanding Russian culture is understanding extreme conditions
and struggles, understanding the significance of soul and the value of
endurance. The terms identified as essential to Russian people—
patience, suffering, extremes, soul, and endurance—cannot be found in
any material objects. To understand how these aspects of Russian culture shape the lives of the unwanted, the marginalized, and the abandoned, one needs to study experiences and viewpoints of Russians
themselves. For this reason, I hold sacred the subjective experiences of
Russians as expressed in conversation, throughout their daily lives and
in interviews.

While in general children are seen as Russia's future, homeless children are symbols of the suffering and victimization of Russia as a
whole. Society perceives them in two ways: as untouchables and as the
underdogs who conform to the Russian legacy of suffering. The greatest of the Russian thinkers and writers have depicted the underdog simultaneously as victim and hero. Both nineteenth-century writers Leo
Tolstoy and Fyodor Dostoevsky convince their readers that even the
most superficially despicable person, when analyzed, is really as human
and understandable as anyone else, given the historical environment to
which he is born. I have chosen Tolstoy and Dostoevsky as examples

because Russians themselves frequently quote these authors to communicate the essence of Russian beliefs.

In Tolstoy's *Death of Ivan Ilyich* and Dostoevsky's *Notes from the Underground*, it is the underdog's suffering that makes him human and brings him closer to the average person. In suffering, people become conscious of life and then become honorable. In discussing his suffering and the value of suffering, the hero of Dostoevsky's *Notes from the Underground* explains:

Maybe suffering is just as profitable for him [the underdog] as well-being? . . . As for my personal opinion, to love just well-being alone is somehow indecent. . . . Suffering—why, this is the soul cause of consciousness.[25]

In *The Death of Ivan Ilyich*, Tolstoy depicted the hero as attaining consciousness only in death: "Ivan Ilyich's life had been most simple and most ordinary and therefore most terrible." As Ivan Ilyich becomes depressed in sickness, while hated by the average equal in his social surroundings for his anger and contempt, he ceases to be ordinary or most terrible.

Vladimir Nabokov characterized Tolstoy's story of Ivan's death as really the story of his "Life." Ivan Ilyich had lived a bad life because he was concerned only with the superficial and materialistic. "Since a bad life is nothing but the death of the soul, then Ivan lived a living death, and since beyond death is God's living light, then Ivan died into a new Life. Life with a capital L."[26] The suffering underdog is actually closer to God and thus valued by Russians and recognized as a true Russian, a martyr. A Russian can, at the same time, shun and identify with the outcast as him or herself.

Hardships faced by Russians today are extreme. They appear as horrendous to the outside world and insurmountable to those living them. Russians have not grown immune to the misery they encounter. Instead, they suffer it daily as they venture onto the streets in their quest for a "normal" life. Their suffering is expressed in their reactions to the beggar on the street: sighs of disapproval, laments, and scolding. Yet personal instability and lack of help from outsiders or the government forces most Russians to turn their backs on an other's misery.

In my experience, a Russian's emphasis on suffering as intrinsic to "Russianness" has assisted the growing crisis of homelessness. It is not that Russians do not want to help the homeless, but that their own suffering prevents them from being able to reach out to others. Many are sapped of energy and financial resources and physically find themselves unable to help. Others believe that it is not their job or place to help the homeless, but rather the government's. How can one individual Russian make a difference to homelessness in Russia, a problem created by the government, the authority, and one so great that it can only be fixed by an entity as powerful as the government itself? Finally, there are those who believe that the suffering experienced by homeless children is proof that the collapse of the Soviet regime was a bad thing—"After all, under Stalin for example, we had no homelessness."[27] I will challenge this belief in Chapter 3.

Chapter 3

Many Forms of Abandonment

INTRODUCTION TO ABANDONMENT

The term "abandonment" in Russia is rather complex. It is a culturally relative term that may imply characteristics of both the abandoned and the abandoner. Being abandoned may stigmatize the individual, depending on the culture. Both in English and in Russian there are many different terms used to identify abandoned children. When one factors in the children's views of what it means to be abandoned, it becomes clear that in order to understand abandonment, it is best to focus on those directly involved, from the social workers to the children themselves.

Historically, when parents abandoned their children, it was often the result of necessity. While today abandoned children are marginalized, there was a time when this was not the case. During the Leningrad blockade, which began in 1941, the Germans surrounded the city for 900 days, thus hindering any products or necessary materials from entering the city and stopping anyone trying to leave the city. To survive, people ate everything they could, including their pets. More than 641,000 people died of either starvation or disease during this time. Children were often left without a family. One blockade survivor, Lena D., now a grandmother, dressed modestly in gray and brown old clothes, her deep-set wrinkles and lack of teeth alluding to her past suffering, tells her story:

I was one of the lucky ones. I got sick. Everyone in Leningrad was dying of hunger and freezing to death. On January 6, 1942, I had an accident. It was my turn to get bread. I took our four ration tickets (by this time we received a bit more than 125 grams). I had just eaten the little piece and was already entering our yard, when some hand grabbed the bread. I held on and did not let go of it. The next thing I knew, I felt a horrible strike on my head. I ran home with blood in my eyes. Mama was very frightened and immediately took me to the hospital on the 14th tram line. There they wrapped my head with a bandage, so that my hat barely fit. It hurt quite a bit, but I was very proud: I was wounded like a soldier on the front. The doctor who looked in on me was so weak himself that he could barely wrap my bandage around my head, and simply told Mama what to do.

In a few days I fell extremely ill. My head was infected and my eyes nearly closed. . . . Father went to the hospital to fight for a bed for me and by the evening everything had been arranged. The next day, Mama took me to the Krupskaya children's hospital on a sled.

My room was large and dark. I did not receive dinner that night, since I had not been expected. I did not know that and was very angry. The hospital was warm and clean. We received food three times a day, usually semolina made with water. I was impressed by the way the doctors went around in clean, white robes and were happy.

My diphtheria ended and my head did not hurt anymore, but for some reason no one came to pick me up. Why was no one talking about letting me go home? Almost all the children in my room had returned home but I continued to lie there. All these thoughts came to me one night and I could not sleep. In the morning, when my porridge was served, I suddenly realized that Mama had died! That's why all are silent! That's why no one was picking me up! I felt a lump in my throat and I could not swallow, could not even think about food! My tears began to flow and I cried: "My mama, my mama has died because of this porridge! She did not have enough and she died!"

On May 15 a fat, quiet nanny came for me. I was taken to an orphanage. . . . I was taken to orphanage number 32 on the 10th line. As soon as my documents were filled out, I ran home. The doors of our apartment were open and everything had been thrown around. There was no Mama, no sisters. I could not stay, grabbed my doll and ran out of the empty, horrifying house. At night I took the doll to bed, but by the morning, she had disappeared.

There were 115 children, beginning at the infant level in the orphanage. I felt lonely all the time, lost and insignificant. We ate three times a day. We were given soybean candy with our tea. Everything went by rules and often some officials would come to see if we were being fed properly.

My group teacher, Natalya Alexandrovna, saw that I had a hard time getting used to the orphanage and kept me close to her. She began corresponding with my father, when he had found me, and helped me find my sister Katya so that we could be evacuated together. I was thankful and tried to be a good girl.

At the beginning of August we were all evacuated. . . . Having heard that orphans from Leningrad had arrived, residents of Tol'skii Madan immediately rushed to the village club to where we had been trucked. Everyone tried to feed us greens, carrots, cucumbers, turnips, and peas. The children greedily ate everything and the adults lost control over who ate what. . . . The fresh greens did not agree with our stomachs and we all had diarrhea and many developed skin problems. Those were the results of the Leningrad blockade.[1]

Among the stories I collected, this story of abandonment stands out on a number of levels. For one, it is a part of the story of an abandoned city. Leningrad had indeed been abandoned, as Stalin made no obvious effort to help the city out of its misery. Indeed, the two women I interviewed on the subject felt that Stalin had abandoned them. They were among those who, after this experience, could no longer believe in their leader and began to doubt claims that he was a hero, leading them to a better way of life.

When Lena D. and her fellow orphans entered the village of Tol'skii Madan, they were greeted warmly. This is notable. In contrast to other points in Russian history when orphans were shunned and avoided, during the blockade, pity turned to reaching out and helping the orphans. That is because people knew the children's parents had been victims themselves, innocent and able to care for the children had it not been for the war. In contrast, at other points in history and today, parents of orphans were blamed for abandonment. Abandonment is viewed as negative, an act that declares a parent is unworthy and possibly criminal.

DEFINING ABANDONMENT

When we talk about orphans, street children, homelessness, and abandonment, definitions vary not only among scholars but also among American and Russian laymen. For this reason, this author has felt the need to define the term abandonment as it is used throughout this book. I understand the term abandonment from both American and Russian perspectives. The terms need to be discussed in the context of cultural notions of childhood and the history of childhood and orphanhood in Russia. This contextualization will illuminate Russia's cultural taboos and beliefs about abandoned children today and naturally will lead us to a more comprehensive understanding of the lives of orphans.

It is difficult to choose a single label to define all the children who are the subject of this book. "Orphan" befits only a percentage of the children, since the word "orphan" implies that the child has no legal parents. "Street children" is limited to those who live on the streets or who spend most of their lives on streets, who call the streets their home. This term is rather unspecific, as well, varying from one country to the next. In Brazil, for example, a street child is defined as a poor child who is simply in the wrong place at the wrong time.[2] To what extent street children have severed their ties with the family or whether they have another home remains questionable. Finally, the concept of "street child" excludes the institutionalized orphans.

I have tried to focus on all levels of street children and orphans. I use the terms carefully, keeping the complexity of each term in mind. Often, I simply refer to the children as abandoned, since they have been abandoned, either morally or physically, by society or by their families.

However, by using the term "abandoned," I realize the issues I raise. The term suggests a forlorn, neglected, and potentially abused child. These connotations may evoke pity, which, while most often warranted, does not necessarily lead to appropriate action. Abandoned children require help based on thoughtful, scholarly, and sensitive judgment, not on knee-jerk responses. Abandoned means many things. For example, we must understand that for whatever reason, a child might appear to have been physically abandoned, when, in fact, the child herself chose to abandon her family to escape emotional abuse at home.

Moreover, many abandoned children are "home-based," that is, they return home for food and shelter at will or as is acceptable to their families. Thus the term "abandoned" does not necessarily include only children who are completely without material or emotional support. Some of the abandoned have some form of shelter but due to abuse, alcoholism, or an array of other issues, do not live the traditional family life.

I am also aware of the emotional value that is attached to the term, that is, it carries the connotation of sadness, neediness, and hopelessness. This meaning obscures the fact that some abandoned children feel quite hopeful about their lives. While it is indeed difficult to imagine any positive experience in the life of an abandoned child, recent research suggests that survival of the street child or orphan is in itself empowering and that the terms historically used to identify such children have merely discriminated against and acted to demoralize those children.

In the book *Abandoned Children*, edited by Catherine Panter-Brick and Malcolm Smith, contributing authors Angela Veale, Max Taylor, and Carol Linehan argue that the labels themselves have marginalized children and caused people to see them as "abnormal" and in need of serious intervention to "normalize" them. Especially when street children are perceived as a nuisance or a problem, authorities tend to punish the children or try to make them behave "normally."[3] However, as Taylor and Linehan point out, children who choose to live on the streets do so because it gives them something in return, thereby reinforcing their desire to live on the streets.[4] Some homeless children feel empowered by their freedom on the streets and we must keep in mind that not all abandoned children share the same history of helplessness and powerlessness, as has been traditionally assumed in social scientific studies.

My findings have shown that, indeed, orphans and homeless children suffer and feel hopeless, yet they also have a power that comes from their independence. Social scholars have suggested that rather than emphasize the relative powerlessness of individuals in changing political and economic realities, thereby neglecting the power such individuals have in constructing their own cultural world, anthropologists need to look more deeply into the power of survival. One such scholar, Metcalf, writes, "Indeed, they not only can figure out for themselves what sense to make of a world full of rootlessness, alienation, cultural pastiche, and the rest, they *must* do it themselves."[5] The ability to cope, to figure things out, to find food and make shelters, even to create new communities with their own structure and dynamic is proof of the power of the homeless children in Russia.

ABANDONMENT IN RUSSIA

The abandonment of children in Russia has developed as a result of cultural and social circumstances, which, while comparable to other countries that have a noticeable number of street children, is simultaneously unique to Russia. Like Brazil, Russia has experienced social and political turmoil that has led to an unstable and practically nonexistent infrastructure to support and offer aid to homeless children. As in Brazil, the abandonment of children in Russia is a product of sociopolitical and economic instability. According to Scheper-Hughes and Hoffman, slum and street children are victims of social, political, and economic instability.[6] Brazil is not the only example of child victimization and abandonment resulting from social inequalities, and thus, child marginalization can be viewed as a global problem in societies that lack in resources to help street children.

However, marginalization of abandoned children is not only a result of a society's inability to sustain its poor, but also a result of culturally specific beliefs surrounding these children. Stereotyping and stigmatizing are part of Russia's approach to viewing the "other." Erving Goffman defines three different types of stigma: the abominations of the body, blemishes of individual character, and the tribal stigma of race, nation, and religion.[7] Marginalization of children in Russia can be explained by this premise. Indeed children with deformities are often given up to orphanages. Those children who already make a living on the street are commonly perceived to have poor

characters, that is, as being dishonest, treacherous, or emotionally unstable, all characteristics that are "inferred from a known record of,
for example, homosexuality, unemployment, suicidal attempts."[8] As
one shelter director warned me about the homeless children I meet on
the streets, "Don't get too close to the children. You do not really
know them. They don't have any reason to be nice to you unless there
is something in it for them. They have no problem stealing or tricking
you and do not care what you really think."[9]

Finally, a number of children are stigmatized and ultimately abandoned because of their race. Mixed-race children are frequently left
at the doors of orphanages. Goffman goes on to point out that once a
person is stigmatized, he is regarded as not quite human.[10] In Russia,
a stigmatized child, such as an orphan or a street child, is seen as possessing a hopeless fate, which could stigmatize the child's family as
well. An adult may choose to treat "it" as "not quite human" simply
because the child affects the adult in a negative way, that is, he may
cause the adult and the family to be stigmatized and marginalized as
well.

The result is discrimination of the child, through which the child's
life chances are reduced. Russian adults "construct a stigma-theory,
an ideology to explain his inferiority and account for the danger he
represents."[11] Labels for street children or "stigma terms" are commonly used in Russia without giving thought to the original meaning.
As mentioned earlier, what to call the children in question has been
debated in recent anthropological scholarship. Scheper-Hughes and
Hoffman describe how "poor kids on the loose" used to be viewed as
potential cheap labor, but how, with urbanization, they have gained
the reputation of being scandalous, a public nuisance, and a danger:
"This shift is reflected in the stigmatizing terms of reference by which
poor children on the loose are known."[12] Such terms in Brazil include
moleque, which connotes pity for the child and blame for the mother;
marginal, which connotes danger; and *street child*, which may connote an array of meanings such as "illegitimately occupying public
space" or something abnormal.[13]

Even more recent literature confirms the complexity of the problem of labeling abandoned children. Catherine Panter-Brick affirms
that generally, street children are seen as "at risk," that is, as victims,

but also as deviants.[14] In agreement with earlier writings of Goffman, anthropologists today acknowledge that stigmatizing terms have aversely affected the hopes, dreams, and future of abandoned children by marginalizing them. The terms themselves affect how people view abandoned children.

ABANDONMENT TERMINOLOGY IN RUSSIA

In Russia, terms used to refer to homeless children are no less stigmatizing. The most common term used is "беспризорники" (*besprizorniki*) or "беспризорные" (*besprizornye*), translated best as homeless child, waif, or stray. The root of the word, "призор" (*prizor*), refers to that which is tended to or not neglected. It is more frequently used with the word "without" (bez/s) in front of it to mean untended and neglected.

Other terms include "заброшенные дети" (*zabroshennye deti*), meaning neglected children or children who are thrown out, and "бездомные дети" (*bezdomnye deti*), homeless children. Another less standard label is "уличные дети" (*ulichnye deti*), street children. The latter two are perhaps the most derogatory, since the initial word "street" or "homeless" is often paired with dogs as well. Homeless dogs are a rising issue on the streets of Moscow and St. Petersburg, one that is viewed with disdain and embarrassment. Both street children and street dogs are seen as signs of third world status, with all its problems of poverty and powerlessness.

A more recent, more colloquial, and perhaps more significant term than any of the aforementioned is "маленький БОМЖ" (*malen'kii BOMZH*), the latter word being an acronym for "Безопределённого места жительства" (*bezopredelionnogo mesta zhitelstva*), which means "without a fixed residence" and sounds like the English word "bum." They are thus identified as little bums. While the term accurately describes the absence of a real home, it also connotes poverty, despair, dirt, and an inability to fit into the social system. It is yet another term that marginalizes the children in question.

Russians think of "хулыган" (*khuligan*), a hooligan, "шпана" (*shpana*), also a term for hooligan or ruffian, and "дети которые ходят стаями" (*deti kotorye khodyat stayami*), or children who go in packs, as worthy of fear. Even if they have parents and homes, these children are officially termed *"besprizorniki,"* *"BOMZHy,"* and "безнадзорники" (*besnadzorniki*), meaning neglected children. All of these terms arouse unease and even fear in Russian citizens. As one woman concludes in our discussion of terminology, "For me, the word for such children is for the devil and the only emotion I have is an uncontrollable fear of them."[15]

From the Russian child's perspective, labels such as *"besprizorniki"* and others of abandonment and homelessness are also viewed as negative and denigrating. As Goffman predicts, "the stigmatized individual tends to hold the same beliefs about identity that we do. . . . The stigmatized's deepest feelings about what he is may be his sense of being a 'normal person,' a human being, like anyone else, a person, therefore, who deserves a fair chance and a fair break."[16] Russian abandoned children understand their humanness and their rights to be treated as other Russian citizens, but they also understand that they are not generally perceived that way by the nonabandoned.

As with terms used for street children of Brazil, terms described in this chapter have encoded in them a sense of alarm and that something is wrong. The result is a sense of the Russian abandoned child as abnormal, which, in turn, at times leads to inappropriate intervention. As in Brazil, Russian homeless children are placed in overcrowded shelters, jails, and even psychiatric facilities that are unprepared to care for these minors.

As has been pointed out numerous times in social scientific literature, children have a different perspective than an adult on terms of abandonment, street children, and orphans. This riff compounds problems adults face when trying to help such children; an absence of mutual understanding impedes communication as each party resists the other's intentions and actions. Instead, the adult is faced with a suspicious child, and the child sees herself confronted with a combative adult.

In an article by Hecht, the problem of definition is made clear. As a social anthropologist conducting research on street children in Brazil, he thought it logical to ask the children to tell him, in their own words, the difference between "home" and "street." This question assumed that street children in Brazil agreed with his definition of the street child as one who lives on the street as opposed to in the home. It also assumed a traditional definition of the home. Only after some time did Hecht come to understand the children's "blank stares." Unlike Hecht, street children differentiate themselves from other children by a difference in their family relationships rather than by the physical space of the street and the home. Hecht explains:

As poor Brazilians will tell you, one can grow up "in the street" without ever spending a night on the pavement. . . . For the children who sleep in the street in Recife, an essential element that distinguishes them from other poor children is their relationship to a mother figure, be it their biological mother or another woman who raises them—grandmother, stepmother, godmother, aunt or unrelated foster mother. Home and the street are not concepts attached primarily to physical spaces; they are notions revolving largely around the children's relationship to their mother and what they see as the implications of this relationship. Being at home is sustaining a relationship with one's mother, even if the physical space called "home" is nothing more than a few makeshift walls under an overpass, the same type of physical space where children might sleep with their peers but unaccompanied by their mothers.[17]

Similarly, Hecht assumed in his initial questions that home implies family, when home to the street child implies something else:

"[H]ome" is far more than physical proximity to one's mother: it implies, first and foremost, "helping" one's mother, doing in the home the things that she wants done, accepting her advice and discipline, and augmenting the family income or even supplying it entirely.[18]

In this example, we see some of the problems faced when one's basic premise, the terms one employs, are viewed from different perspectives. As a result, the adult trying to communicate with the child is faced with miscommunication, misunderstanding, and, ultimately, stalemate.

The children interviewed for this book generally do not speak of themselves as abandoned, unless the subject is broached. Among themselves, topics of conversation do not center around self-pity, but rather around survival and determination. Much time is spent on how to get around rules: rules of the home, if there were any; rules of the classroom; rules of the school; rules of their institution, be it an orphanage or a shelter; and rules of society. Life for the abandoned child is about bending and avoiding social law, since following the law is perceived by children as stifling and to their disadvantage. Asking the children about abandonment elicits responses of anger and shame, feelings that are quickly suppressed and expressed in their routine behavior of beating the system.

A BRIEF HISTORY OF ABANDONED CHILDREN IN RUSSIA

We can trace the history of shame and marginalization in association with abandonment of children in Russia historically to the tsarist regime. Even in the process of establishing resolutions to the orphan problem in 1712, Peter I (1672–1725) referred to them as "children of shame," a result of the sins of their mothers: Many of these children were abandoned due to illegitimacy and/or poverty. In order to avoid the "still greater sin of murder" of such children, Peter I established hospitals to care for the foundlings.[19]

Under Catherine II (1762–1796), these hospitals became more school-like, teaching children morality, civic mindedness, and respect for authority in the hopes of making working citizens out of the unwanted children. At this point in history, the education of these children was based on the Western philosophical notion that the mind at birth was a blank slate, "possessing no inborn inclinations to evil or vice."[20] The sins of their parents made children shameful, not because of their genetic makeup. Unwed mothers faced humiliation and financial ruin.

Fear of social marginalization led many a mother either to abandon her child on the street, murder her child, or keep the child she did not want, rather than register him as illegitimate.[21] Remaining with parents who did not want them led to poor upbringing and has been heralded as one of the reasons for the rise in the incidence of juvenile delinquency.[22]

Under the Soviet regime, marginalization and even condemnation of abandoned children continued. Russians did not accept homeless children as true Russians, but saw them as outcasts, "not one of ours"—"*ne svoi.*" The concept of "*svoi*" and "*ne svoi,*" that which is "ours" or "not ours," is one that permeates all strata of Russian society and various periods of Russian history. Even within the ranks of street children, new arrivals were considered *ne svoi*. "Regarded as outside the pale (*ne svoi*) by hardened adolescents, many a novice found himself stripped of his clothing and beaten by a group whose path he crossed."[23] These streetwise veterans (*shpany*) lead a society with social stratification, rank, and order of street children, separate from the adult world, that extended into the institutions created to protect victims of abandonment.

The problem of homeless children grew in the 1920s, which gave rise to street gangs. As street gangs developed in proportion, so did problems of juvenile delinquency and crime. Once on the street, even the most well-intentioned child was lured into petty theft. The result was an even greater disdain by the general public, as the image of the poor waif was also that of a petty thief.[24] Emotions toward these "waifs" included condemnation along with fear, revulsion, and pity. Even when the abandoned children were not actually stealing, people were concerned. Their appearance, dirty and dressed poorly, sometimes even in newspaper, caused people to turn away as often as it evoked pity.[25] The result of such emotions was a view of street children as "malignant" and unredeemable.

Comments about the inability to rehabilitate such children came not only from the average Soviet citizen, but from education officials as well. In Baku, a former Soviet city, now the capital of Azerbaijan, the chair of the Juvenile Affairs Committee proclaimed in the early 1920s, "When all is said and done, you will not make a human being out of a *besprizornyi,*"[26] and a police official was overheard calling *besprizornye* a hopeless bunch: "The sooner all your *besprizorniki* die, the better."[27] These children were ultimately labeled as "defective." Common assumptions in facilities dedicated to the care of homeless children included their "moral defectiveness" (*moral'no defektivnost'*), which stems from the "child's own psychological defects rather than from outside influences."[28]

In the late nineteenth and early twentieth centuries, education reformers debated whether juvenile delinquency was a result of innate evil inclinations brewing in some children or the result of external forces such as poverty. The Soviet regime heralded the notion that the bourgeoisie and its descrimination had led to the neglect of children. However, most people subscribed to the belief that inborn negative tendencies drove certain children to lives of delinquency. "Beasts," "damned bandits," and "impossible to mold into human beings" persisted as labels for street children.

In the course of the development of the socialist regime, new party members more frequently began to concur with the public's view: "How could it [a Soviet community] be faulted for those hooligans who endured to blemish an otherwise dazzling vista?"[29] Under the Soviet regime, government leaders would not permit homelessness, and crime of any kind was seen as the fault of the criminals, young and old.

The result was harsh action against all street children, which included prisonlike institutionalization and, according to one informant, "execution of those caught stealing or found infected with venereal diseases."[30] While execution is not commonly practiced at the time of writing this book, the view of abandoned children as "misfits" continues to this day.[31]

THE CONCEPT OF A RUSSIAN CHILDHOOD

In Russia, as in many societies, childhood is revered as a sacred time of life, one that is important to the development of both the individual and society. For Russians, childhood is a socially constructed concept that is connected to cultural notions of the past and the future of the motherland. Historically, the concept of a Russian childhood developed out of the teachings and writings of Leo Tolstoy. As has been elaborated upon in Russian literary scholarship, specifically in the work of Andrew Wachtel, the founding myth of the ideal Russian childhood may have emerged from Tolstoy's writings.[32]

It was in 1852 that Tolstoy published the first part of *Childhood*, a story that introduces readers to an ideal view of an aristocratic childhood in nineteenth-century Russia. While on the one hand a fictional piece, Tolstoy's work is also in part autobiographical. Tolstoy himself described the work as "an incoherent jumble of events from (my

friends') childhood and my own."[33] However, it was also influenced
by nineteenth-century Western philosophers and, like the philosophers of nineteenth-century Europe, Tolstoy affected the ideals and
beliefs of Russians.

Specifically, Tolstoy related in his book a childhood filled with
warmth and happiness. He reminisced in his chapter on childhood:

Oh the happy, happy, never-to-be-recalled days of childhood! How could
one fail to love and cherish memories of such a time? Those memories re-
fresh and elevate the soul and are a source of my best enjoyment.[34]

Russian literature has historically played a vital role in the formation of a Russian worldview and ideology. Beginning in the nineteenth and continuing throughout the twentieth century, Russians
reacted to and were stimulated by their authors. This complex interaction of ideas, attitudes, and beliefs has influenced moral, political,
and spiritual tendencies in Russian society.

Literature has also affected cultural views and political beliefs.
Specifically Tolstoy's *Childhood* sparked responses among even the
most powerful politicians, including Trotsky: "Trotsky's dialogue
with Tolstoy points to a common pattern in Russian cultural history:
in the course of time, a theme or idea first expressed in a work of literature ceases to be a mere literary problem and becomes a sociocultural myth."[35] Tolstoy's childhood gave the Russians a "coherent
integral model" for the definition of childhood as a stage of life that
was then to be culturally defined.[36]

Tolstoy's concept of childhood was itself influenced by a number
of Western writers. These include, but are not limited to, Laurence
Sterne, Henri Rousseau, and Charles Dickens.[37] Like Rousseau, Tolstoy saw childhood as the most happy and pure time of life, or "joyous innocence," as he called it.

In truth, Tolstoy himself had a less joyous experience. His mother
died in 1830, the year that Tolstoy turned two. His father died in 1837.
He was educated and raised by his tutors, living with numerous female
relatives and his four siblings. Nevertheless Tolstoy in *Childhood* im-
parted on the mother a profound role, that of nurturer. He wrote:

Having run about to your heart's content you sit in your high chair at the tea-table. It is late, you have long ago finished your cup of milk with sugar in. So sleepy that you cannot keep your eyes open, still you do not stir from your place but sit and listen. And how can you help listening? Mamma is talking to someone and the sound of her voice is so sweet, so warm. Just the sound of it goes to my heart![38]

In this paragraph, Tolstoy related the experience of the hero of the book to all children, using the general second person singular "you" in his depiction of his memory, as though all children could imagine the moment. Tolstoy thereby drew in the reader, asking him to identify with the hero.

Childhood remained a fascination for Tolstoy, both from philosophical and psychological perspectives. In *Childhood*, Tolstoy documented not only the days of a boy's childhood, but also the "operations and growth of the conscious mind at various stages of development."[39] His interest in the child's mind and pedagogy led him to found a school at Tolstoy's ancestral estate, Yasnaya Polyana, where he worked to teach peasant children. From his own experiences at home and abroad, Tolstoy came to believe that children from different social backgrounds require different means of education to learn the basics of reading, writing, and arithmetic. Yasnaya Polyana, for example, allowed children to work with their parents when needed on the farm and also to attend school as they saw fit, while at the same time preserving the innocence and gaiety of childhood through freedom in the classroom. The experiment was not as successful as Tolstoy had hoped, although some individual stories attest to the possibilities of his philosophy.

The myths of childhood created by Tolstoy had lasting effects on Russian literature and society. Before Tolstoy's work, no one had attempted to write from the perspective of the child. According to Wachtel, "before 1852 there were practically no first-person accounts of childhood in Russia."[40] The idealistic meaning of childhood as described by Tolstoy lead to the affirmation of the proper childhood, one that was aspired to by not only authors, but parents and educators as well:

In effect, then, Tolstoy created what could be called the myths of Russian childhood, myths that were developed and canonized not in fiction but in autobiography. The Tolstoyan myths of childhood became so strongly embedded in the Russian cultural mind that they could not be ignored, even by those members of the gentry class who had had unhappy childhoods and by writers from other classes. . . . Thus, the interpretation of childhood that Tolstoy proposed in *Childhood* became both a literary and sociocultural theme in Russia.[41]

Wachtel's conclusion that Tolstoy's childhood myths prevailed throughout the Soviet years further complicates the lives of those less fortunate, those with unhappy childhoods. Due to the ideal standard set by Tolstoy, many Russians feel that they have missed out on a good and proper childhood.

As reflected both in historical and literary accounts of childhood and abandonment, families with abandonment in their history were not acceptable to the Russian way. Today, this ideal childhood has become so ingrained in the minds of Russians that any other childhood seems deficient. As a result, children exposed at an early age to the adult Russian world, with all its trials and tribulations, may be viewed as underprivileged and lacking in certain ways. When children do not fit the idealized concept, such as in the case of orphans, they become marginalized and abandoned, finding it difficult to integrate into the adult world as they grow up. Abandonment is thus not only conducted by families but by society as a whole.

Abandonment is not only conducted by adults, it is experienced by adults. Since the collapse of the Soviet regime, Russians have experienced loss: loss of stability, loss of predictability, and loss of security. Many Russians interviewed feel abandoned by their leaders and by their society. Покинутый (*pokinutyi*), abandoned or thrown out, is a term often expressed by Russians to describe themselves. It is also a term used to refer to the act of leaving or abandoning one's homeland. The concept of having been abandoned is deeply linked to a sense of victimization felt by many Russians. From the studies conducted on laments and litanies, we find that in daily conversation, the feeling of victimization is expressed frequently and is seen in collected examples of daily conversation that demonstrate the pervasiveness of feelings of not only victimization but also of abandonment. Professor of Pedagogy Irina S. laments, "We are experiencing what I think you call a 'brain drain.' All of our intelligentsia are gone or moving! Only a few of us are left behind. And look with whom we are left! It is a nightmare." Similarly, Ries documents one Russian man as saying:

Yes, you know, I am thirty-five years old and I am part of a lost generation. We are all, those people of my age, a lost generation. There was nobody to teach us, to pass on the wisdom of the past. Our teachers did the best they could, but so much was lost, that when it came to us, we suffered under a real lack.[42]

This sense of abandonment plays a critical role in creating a sense of shared identity. Yet this shared identity also leads to the notion that victimization is an experience of fate that cannot be changed.

The notion of abandonment runs deep in Russian society and is a frequent lament, affecting not only how people think of themselves, but how they treat their surroundings. In action, Russians express the sentiment, "If no one cares for me, then I cannot be bothered with others or anything not personal." A certain carelessness toward public and impersonal spaces has gone so far as to affect the state of public places, including the environment. As we shall see in the next chapter, this lack of care of the environment and others has come full circle to once again victimize the most vulnerable: the children.

Chapter 4

Moscow's Homeless Children

BACKGROUND

We—my husband, my children, our pets, and I—moved to Moscow in 1998. It was time for me to study street children, to understand the extent to which abandonment happens in Russia and to get to know the children themselves as individuals.

It was not difficult to locate street children. It seemed that throughout my daily routine, there they were: at the markets, in the parks, or at the metro stations, sitting on cardboard, rummaging through garbage, or begging at the stands. I could not guess their ages: Were they four or nine? Ten or fifteen? On the one hand, they appeared malnourished and small, on the other hand, their faces seemed older, tougher than they should at their age. Most of them had dirty faces and hands, apparently sticky from the glue they had been sniffing. Their eyes seemed unfocused, never looking straight into another's eyes, like the shy, stray dogs that shared their space and lurked in the corners, greedily devouring scraps from the filthy ground. So these were the children I planned to meet and to understand. At first the project seemed impossible because, while it was not difficult to find these children, approaching them felt more precarious and uncertain.

As I stepped back from the crowds and took the time simply to watch, I observed how they approached each other fearlessly and compassionately, often sharing food or cigarettes in a way that they did not interact with adults. In their company, I soon sensed a hidden power among them. This power was unlike the relationship of the young institutionalized children. This was a different world, separate from the adult world. I discovered increasingly a rift that exists between the adult world and that of the street children. From the Russian adult's perspective, I learned that while Russian parents and educators believe in certain principles of education that apply to all children, in practice, not all children are valued as equals. The ideal concept of childhood as a stage in life untainted by adult problems does not apply to street children. Even though Russian parents and educators view childhood as potentially the most joyous time of life, children abandoned by their families are victims of Russia's social crisis, and while they find strength among themselves, they barely survive on a day-to-day basis. Relatively few adults concern themselves with the future of these children. The infrastructure to support these children is lacking and, in some cases, absent. As a result, a rising number of children seek solace among themselves, in groups and gangs.

The mistrust and contempt that exists between homeless children and the adult world can be traced back to Stalin's rule during the 1920s when, due to hunger and abandonment, thousands of children took to the streets as they do today. Many of these children spent little time begging and quickly discovered benefits in stealing. One study conducted from 1925 to 1928 found that the likelihood for children to take to theft largely depended on whether or not they came from the city. The children, who moved quickly from begging to stealing, more often came from urban families than from country homes.[1] Furthermore, the longer a child remained homeless, the more likely he or she was to become a petty thief. Thus marked as potential thieves, homeless children were despised by adults and ultimately shunned.

Already in the 1920s, in turn, homeless children, had little faith in their surrounding adult society. Collections of interviews with and stories about homeless youth in the 1920s depict the children's hatred of the adult world. Adults to such children represented merely "potential victims or persecutors."[2] Already in the 1920s, these children had lost their childhood to society. No longer open to adult care and no longer hoping for true empathy, street children found power in taking advantage of the adult world, which, in their minds, only hindered their potential. Homeless children believed in, as they do now, the reproach proclaimed in one of their songs entitled "And Now My Soul Is Hardened."[3]

As children on the streets of urban Russia struggle to survive, they bring to their experience fragments of a childhood so treasured by children with homes. As children with homes build secret hideaways in backyards, so homeless children treasure their clandestine world separate from adults.

Today's Russian children continue to build their headquarters amid the adult world: behind garages, in backyard boxes, in sheds and dark corners, in bushes and tree branches. A Russian youth member recalls:

So here is the kind of headquarter we had when I was about seven to eight years old . . . we met at our headquarters (in the backyard), told scary stories, jokes, played cards, and watched all the people through a split between the boards. It was interesting, since no one could see us. We sat there for hours.

Another youth remembers:

Our headquarter was made of sticks. There were real corridors in it, closed off by branches and polyethylin planks. The branches were quite low. We had to crawl on our hands and knees, stopping at fallen branches. They became benches. The headquarter was a place of discovery and of organizing "war plans." Adults knew about it and constantly chased us away from there, but the headquarters would be rebuilt again. At about the age of seven, a neighbor and I built a house-shelter. It was made of some plants with long stalks of about two and a half meters. To this day I do not know what kind of plants those were and how we got them. With long ropes we wove these long stalks with big leaves and bound them together. In effect, we had a shelter with no light. In it we felt comfortable and warm. It was "our" place, and no one knew about it. We collected berries and made "evening dinners" and ate it all ourselves.

Another boy reminisces:

Our shelter was under the stairs in the entrance hall. It was made of boxes and everyone had their own room in which was a "library," "television," "weapons," and a "headquarter's plan." It was a place where we kept secrets, a place which we valued. The goal of the club was the club itself. Why we built it, we did not understand.

Others remember as well:

For headquarters we built huts. In the winter we constructed them out of discarded Christmas trees, in the summer out of boxes, branches, sticks. Most important: the existence of secrets. Members of the game had a call sign, we had scenarios, strictly assigned roles, and everyone had a self thought-up name. As a rule, there were imagined enemies. For example, we, the Indians, they [chance passers-by] the pale faced. The hut was our own world, standing in contrast to everything else.[4]

As the yards and parks offer a place for children to create their own secret world, the streets offer an opportunity for homeless children to develop their own version of a secret childhood, filled with specifically child traditions. Because of their interaction with the streets and parks, Russian children, unlike children in U.S. cities, are perhaps more intrinsically part of the urban landscape. Unlike in New York parks, in Moscow parks, children's club houses or club headquarters (*shtaby*) are easily discovered in trees and bushes. Child street culture is and historically has been pervasive in Russian cities.

Children's secret headquarters can be characterized in numerous ways: by type of shelter, gender of children, age group, and family background of children. However, whether these shelters are made of wood or boxes or belong to homeless children or children with secure families, they all carry similar initial motivations of the children: to separate themselves as much as possible from the adult world and to create a special place for themselves outside the boundaries of adult interest and influence and to assume a communal identity of "we" as belonging and sticking together.

A secret language usually accompanies the creation of special headquarters. All children, abandoned or not, have a certain predilection for codes, signs, and secret symbols and signals. Secret languages are passed along from generation to generation of children and are an inherent part of child culture. Children have a desire to master secret languages, which they share among themselves. This language helps children develop as members of a youth community. Languages, codes, and secrets help children not only in their personal growth, but also in their gaining independence from adults.

Language is a means by which children develop a sense of communitas. From a psychological perspective, it is important for every child to identify with and feel support from other children. Children experience the development of the self by identifying with a group of children through which, in turn, they become a part of that special world of child culture. Child culture offers the child an acknowledgment, sense of self, and, in effect, empowerment. The described headquarters may be understood as a form of the self: a form of self-affirmation as part of child culture, apart from the peripheral adult world, detached, secret, inaccessible to anyone else, a special independent world that appears as a symbolic epicenter of child life.[5]

For street children in particular, this epicenter functions to support the natural desire for children to maintain what little power and autonomy they have. Becoming a part of a secret culture gives children the power of resistance and subversion. This subversive quality is created by a desire of children to build their own structured society in which they can experiment with being "bad" or "disobedient."[6] For homeless children, power through subversion is especially important, as it serves to maintain their lives. It is a means of survival.

The fact that homeless children have found power in each other's company is not to suggest that they do not desperately need help. The problem is that in the past, help offered by the Russian government has been less than a small bandage to cover a deep wound. These children need more than a cold room, hard bed, and minimal food. These children function on a much deeper level and have chosen power in street culture over the life offered in institutions. Only with a better understanding of these children on a cultural and psychological level can proper care be instituted.

SOME FACTS

Generally, Russian adults require that homeless children live on adult terms by forcing them to subsist as adults, in an adult world, by earning a living, yet unlike adults, by taking only menial jobs. Homeless children have fewer options as to what they can do to make money. While children are initially able to get by on the streets of Moscow, their days are numbered. Some children set out to earn a living by cleaning cars or by rummaging through garbage. This money is often used to pay for food and shelter for their families. One boy interviewed was told by his father that he was not allowed to spend the night at home if he did not return with a bottle of vodka. Suffering due to their parents' addictions, many children simply run away.

This generation of abandoned children may already be lost to a life of panhandling, narcotics, petty theft, and prostitution. As Stoecker points out, "Homelessness and juvenile crime are related phenomena, and many criminologists and sociologists call homelessness the 'mother' of juvenile crime."[7] According to Stoecker, the bleaker the situation of the child, the more serious the crime he or she is likely to commit. "Simply put, hunger causes theft of food; lack of shelter and food leads to serious theft; and lack of shelter combined with unemployment is a precursor of prostitution among girls."[8] Statistics show that in one region of Russia, Primorskii Krai, "one out of every ten youths becomes homeless."[9] While statistics on homelessness are hard to come by anywhere in the world, it is likely that in Russia, the rising number of homeless is correlated to the rising number of children committing crimes.

In jail, children are hardened by the adult criminals around them: "[O]ccasionally these youths are placed in closed institutions with those who have committed more serious crimes, even rape or murder."[10] According to an informer who spent a number of months in prison on a drug conviction, the victimization of youths in prisons is inevitable. Due to overcrowding, prisoners spend their days in a large hall, with fewer beds than people. A hierarchy exists that makes it clear who gets to use the beds and when. If a prisoner is at the low end of the totem pole, he becomes the "girl" for those higher in rank. Youths are likely to be raped in prison.

While homeless children are aware of the consequences of crime, they are also aware that by playing into the hands of adults, by allowing themselves to be committed to shelters and orphanages, their quality of life is diminished to the extent that it is worth taking a risk and joining those living on the streets. Many homeless children are not willing to accept help from shelters, which offer little to no emotional comfort and little more than a roof, bedding, and mediocre food. "I earn more on the streets, get better stuff," Alec proclaims. Shelters are used by many only in times of dire need. The children may return many times, but they often leave after a short respite. These children have learned to take only as much as they want and need from adults, leaving any other comforts, such as love or physical and emotional warmth, to be retrieved from their community of homelessness.

A child's view of choosing to live on the streets as opposed to choosing to live in shelters is different from that of adults. A director of a Moscow shelter explains the adult view:

Of course, we cannot keep addicted kids. Since they are already so addicted, they are unwilling to be helped. We cannot help those that do not want to be helped, so we only take them in when it is really cold or wet outside and send them out again the next morning. We only have so many beds, which we keep for those who want our help.[11]

The children I spoke to, on the contrary, felt they were not "rejected" from the shelter as much as they were "released." The adult world does not accommodate the world of the addicted homeless child and, once "set free" from the shelters or other institutions, the only roofs these children may find, besides those of train stations and abandoned buildings, are prisons.

Many homeless children interviewed differ from their adult counterparts in that they still have hopes of a better future. This "better future," however, does not include a mainstream ideal. While they dream of making it big, of earning a lot of money and of being respected, the children I spoke with have their own ideas of how to achieve that goal. Young girls are lured by the United States and other countries and offer their bodies for prostitution in return for a ticket to what they think will be freedom. One option some of the boys believe in is to become a hired killer, preferably by an American. America, to them, is the ideal country for such criminal activity. Alec, an eleven-year-old homeless child, reminds me, "In America life would be better: I could go to Disneyland."

Such a difference in opinion of what a good future entails has much to do with what society has made available in terms of life stories that can work for homeless children. Bourdieu describes how dominant groups may justify their dominance and, in turn, the inferiority of others. The justification is perpetuated as a social myth. This social myth is ingrained in the people's minds via the education and socialization they receive. Bourdieu explains, "A large part of social suffering stems from the poverty of people's relationship to the educational system, which not only shapes social destinies, but also the image they have of their destiny."[12] Dominant groups, via schools and other media, may perpetuate myths that give members of a society ideas of what may be accomplished in a life, depending on one's status in that particular society. While to the dominant group these myths may be enabling, to the dominated, they are limiting. Russian homeless children, in reaction to the negative image of their destiny given to them by the adult world, have taken it upon themselves to beat the system by turning to crime.

Still other children are caught in a complex situation out of which there is no escape. Dima, a serious boy who at first seemed tough and hard to engage in conversation, finally one day told me his story as it had also been told to me by his shelter administrator. At the age of ten, Dima, a Russian, was forced to flee with his family from Kyrghyzstan. With little money and nowhere to go, his father left the family and his baby brother died en route. After many days of living in various train stations, the mother began drinking and attacked a man for his money. She was given a sentence of seven years in prison. Dima, with no papers to allow him into an orphanage in Moscow and no future in his hometown, has nowhere to live. Foster families do not want to welcome him into their homes for fear they may have to deal with his criminal mother. Instead, he spends his nights in a shelter, hoping for a miracle.

Dima's large blue eyes fill with tears as he talks about his mother. "She will come out of jail and we will build a life here." However, when asked to draw a picture of the family he might some day have, it includes himself and two sons. There is no mother. When I point out the absence of a wife or mother in his drawing, Dima seems surprised. "What for? Why do I need a wife? Why do my children need a mother?" This response surprises me, as I know the cultural value that is placed on mothers in Russia. Mothers in Russia are cherished as both the stronghold and the foundation for all that is good about Russia. Russia herself is referred to frequently as "Mother Russia." Dima has not benefited from such traditional Russian beliefs.

Perhaps Dima is lucky that no Russian orphanage will have him. In general, orphanages today do offer adequate shelter and food, but children are often left to fend for themselves when it comes to making emotional attachments to people or objects. Toys and other personal belongings are not kept long, since other children will, in all likelihood, steal or break them. Personal relationships experience a similar destiny: They are difficult to maintain because many children move away and others are mistrusted.

The supervisor of a class in school or in an institution does not have the time or energy that each individual child requires, and psychological counseling, if available, is often poorly developed. Among each other, children often feel competitive with one another for short supplies of food, toys, compassion, and love. The experience of the orphanage is one reason many older children adopted into Western families exhibit an inability to attach to their new families.

Official child institutions do not prepare children for life in society, much less for life in families. In orphanages, children live a regimented life, one in which they are discouraged from making personal decisions. Moreover, children in orphanages are not encouraged to participate in creative activities or to socialize with the outside world. In a study conducted in 1992, Dement'eva concluded that orphans do not know how to realize themselves through relationships due to their regulated environments in the orphanages.

Many children adopted from Russian orphanages have been assessed as having serious emotional problems. Specifically, attachment disorder is one common result of a life lacking a deep relationship with a caregiver. Symptoms of attachment disorder include an inability to give and receive affection, lack of eye contact, indiscriminate affection for strangers, extreme anger, manipulative behavior, stealing, hoarding or gorging food, preoccupation with fire or gore, lack of impulse control and cause and effect thinking, learning and speech disorders, lack of conscience, lying, lack of friends, incessant chatter, and behavior that is inappropriately demanding or clingy.

The problem with the institutions like orphanages, boarding homes, and shelters is that they do not meet the needs of the children in question. There are, however, a few shelters and programs in Moscow that do reach out to the youths in ways that allow the children to flourish not only physically but emotionally as well. While the stories homeless children have to tell are sad and frightening, some children have found help in such special shelters and daytime programs. These institutions are run by adults who are involved because they actually care. Unlike the orphanages, such grassroots organizations are less dependent on the government for funding; indeed, the government chooses to pay them less, thus forcing the shelters to seek help elsewhere—from local businesses, church groups, or foreign not-for-profit organizations. While lack of funding hampers their ability to give the children all they need, it also allows them to treat the children in ways that surpass the treatment children receive in regular orphanages. Adult volunteers and workers in one shelter unanimously agree that traditional orphanages and *internaty* (child boarding homes) are not the best solution for abandoned children.

One shelter in particular, Shelter of Childhood, tries to create a homelike atmosphere by giving the children more personal attention and affection than traditional orphanages provide. Children in this shelter do not fear their teachers and enjoy frequent hugs. Increasingly, shelters are providing children with basic psychological counseling, promoting their return to their families, and, when this is not feasible, placing children in foster care rather than allowing them to vanish in the social vacuum of orphanages.

Grassroots programs, like Maria's Children, an art rehabilitation center for orphans, are few. Maria Yeliseyeva founded this program through which orphans gain a sense of worthiness and belonging.

Due to lack of funding and educational training, programs providing psychological and emotional support are still rare in Russia but very important if these children are to be given an opportunity to survive in the adult social world.

FROM THE PERSPECTIVE OF THE CHILD:
KOLYA'S STORY

The average Russian's perspective on daily life is perhaps quite unlike anything a Westerner has ever considered, yet it is the life that serves as a context for Russian homeless children. This adult life, contrary to many children's lives, is a life that does not question the future, is one that has no space for thoughts about tomorrow, but rather is one that is bound to the here and now and compelled by a need for immediate gratification. A worker, Oleg, described it best:

The majority of the Russian population has nothing to work toward and cannot imagine what there might be to look forward to beyond the next vodka bottle. . . . Since perestroika, even with changes in leadership, nothing has changed in the lives of the average Russian. In Moscow, perhaps. But overall, people struggle for food and warmth, especially in the winter. And once that is achieved, they await their pay, which perhaps comes once a year. . . . And when the pay comes, they don't think about what to do with it. You and I may consider investing in a mobile phone, or something useful, or something for the future, but such thoughts do not enter their minds. Their pay is invested in vodka. And once that vodka is bought, everything is taken care of: Warmth has been obtained, and hunger has been appeased. Life has improved immediately with that vodka. That is their future.[13]

From the perspective of the Russian adult, although addicted to alcohol, being able to destroy physical and emotional pain with vodka, is, in fact, taking control of one's own life.

The need for immediate gratification, measure of control, and immediate cessation of distress is true not only for adults, but for homeless children as well. Like these adults, homeless children are empowered by their ability to meet their physical needs. It all begins with their ability to survive from one day to the next and, on cold days, from one hour to the next. The children take what they can get and devour what they have. Once they have taken care of their most basic physical needs, that is, food and shelter, they look for something to take away the emotional and other physical pain. Drugs and alcohol are, of course, a common solution. These take the children to a warmer state of being, detached from their pain. At one point, when the emotional needs overwhelm the physical, drugs and alcohol take first priority, above food and shelter. The desire for immediate gratification is one force that drives the lives of the homeless children.

Russian homeless children are, on one level, comparable to people in poor countries who appear to simply deal with circumstances that are not in their control and who merely "look out for opportunities when they appear on the horizon."[14] However, also like adults in these countries, homeless children, even in the context of Russian social chaos, are able to construct their own world and, as Metcalf points out in his discussion of marginalized groups, "in this, they are very far from powerless.[15]

I met Kolya, age twelve, through an American volunteer at a soup kitchen. She had taken Kolya into her home and had hopes of adopting him. On one occasion Kolya joined us for a Halloween party at my house. Together with my sons and others, Kolya, a tall, dark-haired boy with eyes that seemed to laugh, romped and played and I delighted in his happiness. Kolya told me about his experience on the streets of Moscow and, more often, at the Yaroslavskii train station. At the train station, he made his living selling flowers through which he was able to make enough money to satisfy his physical hunger:

I'd take them [flowers] from an old lady [*babushka*] and at the end of the day, gave her the money of which she gave me some. I used to earn more than my mother. There were days when I earned sooo much! One day I started late and I earned about 600 rubles [approximately $22.00]! I took myself out to McDonald's, bought myself fries . . . in short, everything!

From these words, we learn that Kolya feels anything but powerless. In fact, he feels he comes out ahead and takes great pride in making more than is needed for immediate gratification.

Kolya is a very proud boy and feels he has his life more together than anyone in his family. Life was rough, but throughout our conversations, he never pitied himself. In fact, compared to other homeless children, he feels he was quite lucky. "There was a six year old with a family. They'd eat the food and give him the rind. I felt sorry for him." Kolya feels lucky that he not only got more than a rind from his family, but that he had a family to begin with. He is very close to his sister, who can do no wrong. Even when caught prostituting herself, Kolya denies her activities.

Kolya, like many of the children I spoke with, refuses to see himself as a victim. Only when remembering the real loss of a loved one does he show sadness, like when his dog was killed. "In the summer sometimes, we lived in a specific park. I had a dog, a purebreed. He was very attached to me. But the police shot him." At this point in the conversation, Kolya becomes quiet and it is hard for him to say much more. We resume our conversation another day.

When not confronted by the powerlessness he feels at the loss of a loved one, Kolya feels strong and intelligent. He feels he is the man with the solutions for his family. In describing his life before Moscow, when he lived in a shack with no running water and no heat, he is adamant that he understands how to save money and live better than his mother:

We did not always live in Moscow. We had a dacha in Ryazan—small, but we lived well. But my mama eats so much, we had to come to Moscow to make money. My mama may be crazy: She always has to eat meat, which is expensive! I told my mother over and over again to buy a cheap house so we could live normally. But no, she wants to save money for an expensive house, so instead, she spends money on meat and again we are left without a place to live! And we have little food! When Mama gives me a plan on how to sell flowers, it never works, but when I make the plan, I make a lot.

Kolya considers himself the wise one in his family and, in a sense, the leader of his family, as contributing his plan on how to survive, as vital to his family's survival. In fact, Kolya is the youngest of three and was unable to save his sister from prostitution and drugs, his brother from drugs and petty theft, and his mother from alcoholism.

PASHA'S STORY

Pasha lived in a home that is worthy of description. I met him in a boarding home that had recently been built by a Finnish company in the hopes of helping homeless children in Russia. The building was enormous: five stories high, made of brick, with long, dark corridors leading to a network of rooms. Each network of rooms served a different function: In one you might find a few bedrooms with ten beds to a room, surrounding a community space, while in another room you might find a therapy center. No rooms were labeled, nor did any maps guide the visitor. One simply had to know where one was going.

My first visit to Pasha's boarding home was eerie, to say the least. I found myself wandering down halls aimlessly in search of the director's office. There were no adults at the entrance and, upon entering, I noticed two young boys following me, hiding behind the large columns every time I turned around. I tried to ask them for directions, but they just giggled and hid. I searched for adults and at one point stumbled into a room only to find a young girl, no more than sixteen years old, kissing her boyfriend in a television room. She was one of the temporary caretakers and it was naptime for her group of five to seven year olds. The little ones were beginning to wake up, so I asked if I could meet them. Overcome by the embarrassment of "getting caught," she quickly led me to the sleeping quarters. Before I could be introduced, one of the girls jumped on her bed and began screaming and pointing at me, "Who are you? A foreigner? A Nazi?" The other children followed her lead and it took quite some effort to calm them down.

I returned to my search for the director's office. I found it tucked away on the fifth floor. The director greeted me and told me of a new development in their program: art therapy. It was through art therapy that I met Pasha, then age ten. Pictures painted by the children hung on the walls of the office, the only brightly lit room in the home. I noticed one painting with brown streaks and a yellow dagger. It was Pasha's. "He has come a long way," the art therapist interjected as I looked at the painting. "Only since he has been painting has he started to come out of his shell and tell us about himself."

I was introduced to Pasha, an insecure yet outwardly defiant child.

I asked if he could give me a tour of his boarding home. Pasha seemed pleased at the idea of leading me, the American, and with pride, he took me to his group's quarters for boys ages nine to twelve. Unlike the quarters for the younger children, this one seemed empty: The only furniture on the dirty linoleum floors were beds and an accompanying nightstand. Nothing but dust was on the nightstands.

I was taken aback by a large black spot in the center of the room, amid the beds. I asked Pasha what it was, to which he replied, "We were bored, so we decided to pretend we were camping and made a fire." "Didn't you get into trouble?" "No one knew. No one watches, really." And so it was. As I got ready to leave, Pasha asked if he could accompany me. "Are you allowed to leave the premises?" I asked. "No, not officially, but no one cares if I do, as long as I am back by bedtime." And so Pasha took me home on the metro.

Pasha lost his parents in a car accident when he was four. His grandmother still works and could not be with him after school, so she gave him to an orphanage. Pasha was notorious for running away and earning a living on the streets. Finally he was taken in by the police and sent to the boarding home to receive counseling. When I met Pasha, he refused to go to school, dreamed of being free and of camping in nature. He loved his grandmother and was convinced that one day she would take him home.

Pasha was, like many of the children I met, strong, that is, tough on the outside and seemingly, yet not really, hardened by his experiences.

I know my grandmother will come and get me. I feel sorry for her. She is so sad and upset that she cannot care for me. I visit her on weekends and that makes her happy. She makes the best *blinye* [Russian pancakes]. She loves to feed me and I love to eat. I don't like it at the boarding home. It is boring. There's nothing to do. And you cannot keep any toys or things. Someone will steal them or break them. If you do have something, it's better to hide it well. Carry it with you and never show or tell anyone about it.

From his own words, it is easy to see that Pasha, like Kolya, feels confident about certain aspects of his life, or at least he talks himself into them. His sadness is apparent in his serious demeanor, but, like his peers, he shows no weakness. He is motivated by his weekly visits with his grandmother, and rather than expressing any sadness about his own life, he transfers his emotions to feeling sorry for a relative, much like Kolya feels the need to take care of his family. With the hope of a future life with his grandmother, Pasha feels empowered and does not let daily life in the boarding home bring him down. Pasha, like many of his peers, lives in his dreams of a better future.

One theme I discovered in my many conversations with homeless children is the yearning for something to own. Whether it be a toy, a car, a bicycle, or a pet, children in shelters bemoan the fact that they had to give up what they once had and that to have anything is precarious: It makes you and the object a target, but it also enhances your status if you are able to keep it. However, most of the children are not as openly concerned about their status as they are with simply owning something.

I found out from his art therapist that Pasha did in fact own something: a small toy car. He had given it to her as soon as he had found it and asked her to keep it for him. She kept it locked away in a special drawer in her room and every so often, Pasha visited with the car simply to see it and to make sure it was still there. The car was their secret and his pride.

Pasha, like many former street children, feels empowered by his ability to take care of himself and by his independence. He notes that it is his grandmother who benefits from their visits, rarely mentioning his own feelings. He enjoys his food, but that is all he will admit. He believes that he is needed, a basic desire by many of the children I interviewed. He would never admit to needing his grandmother; rather, she needs him to be happy.

When you enter an orphanage in Russia, children will run up to you, hug you, hold on to you, sometimes even hurt you so that you will notice them and touch them. The craving for touch by these children is more than any one person can give. When you enter a shelter with former street children, you encounter a similar craving: Children may not grab you, but they may stalk you, carefully come closer and hover around you. These children crave closeness but have the wisdom not to trust simply anyone. Pasha followed or led me everywhere. It was as if he did not want to ever let go of me. He had, through some time, discovered that I could be trusted and that was invaluable to him. He followed me home and begged to stay. I could not let him. He had followed me unofficially and it was dangerous for both of us. He had risked punishment to follow me home. He would risk anything for proximity to someone trustworthy enough.

The pattern relationships take in the lives of such young children as Pasha is not conducive to the establishment of relationships in the future. While there may be good people he meets along the way, none are there to stay. Parents abandon, or, as in Pasha's case, they pass away. Teachers and therapists come and go. I came and went. Pasha quickly learned that no relationships last. Can we expect Pasha himself to commit to relationships in the future?

Studies have shown that children who have suffered a series of episodes in which they have been abandoned or who have been institutionalized often have a hard time bonding with people. Another finding has been that these children attach very quickly but only briefly to complete strangers. It is as if they cannot get too close. For some it is a fear of impending loss of a relationship once closeness has been established and the heart has been opened. For others it is the inability to connect on a deeper level. Indeed, how could they, having never experienced closeness as a child? Instead, they continue to dream, sometimes unrealistically, of a fantasy life.

MASHA'S STORY

Masha lived in a curious home. It was a boarding home in a beautiful, old town outside St. Petersburg. The town is called Pushkin, or formerly known as Tsarskoe Selo (Tsar's village). It had the first Russian railway station in 1837 and was the town in which Pushkin attended a Lycee in 1811. Prior to all this, Peter the Great's wife had chosen the town for her country home and Empress Elizabeth later chose to build a palace there in 1741. Pushkin is known for its fresh air and healthy climate, compared to St. Petersburg. In the early 1900s many children came to resorts in Pushkin to benefit from the environment in the summers. It was so popular for children that at one point (1918) it became known as Detskoe Selo (Children's Village), but it became Pushkin in 1937. Masha's home had been built as a boarding home, one that was to house children who had relatives. Somehow, a street child named Masha found her way here.

When I first met Masha, she was in the large dining hall, eating alone at the table. A teacher and I joined her. She was eating early as she had been excused from class due to a headache. I was informed that the dining hall is not this quiet during lunchtime. In fact, children were quite wild, taking the "good" food from those less able to defend themselves. One teacher explained that children with disabilities can even starve at an orphanage or boarding home, as stronger children steal their food. Masha ate her food at a steady pace, without looking up.

I tried to make eye contact with Masha and succeeded a few days later. She never fully trusted anyone and certainly not the foreigner asking her questions. She was young but strong. A leader, she directed and demanded of others and rarely partook in group activities. She did not like to talk about anything at length, much less herself.

Masha did not really want to talk about the past. At the age of eight she was caught by the police prostituting herself. Her mother was located but not permitted to keep Masha. She was described as an alcoholic with tuberculosis, jobless, and with no means to support her children. Masha did recall one occasion:

All I remember is that it was hard to find food. I started stealing, but never got much. My mother is sick, so I cannot stay with her. She will get me when she is better. When they first brought me to a shelter, I had to live in isolation for a long time and they made me take cold baths a lot. I don't like water on me and cold water especially, but I guess it is better than being cold at night. They shaved my hair off because they said I had lice.

Masha's experience at the shelter she was initially held at is typical. When children arrive at the shelter, they are first placed into quarantine until the medical staff is certain that the child is not ill. Children are kept in isolation from other children, their heads shaved and their bodies scrubbed down. It is a particularly difficult time for many children, as they can hear the others in the shelter but cannot meet them or participate in the games they may see being played outside. They usually do not know what will become of them, as a shelter is supposed to be only temporary until either a guardian can be found or the child is transferred to an orphanage. Foster homes are extremely rare.

Masha does not remember much. She does not know her father but does recall an abusive boyfriend. Masha preferred street life to home life: "I'm much safer on the streets. I have a friend and we help each other find food." Again, helping each other out on the streets is key to survival among the children.

Like Pasha, Masha has faith in those she loves, or more specifically, her mother. Even though the staff at the home described Masha's mother as poor, ill, and incapable of ever taking care of Masha, Masha tells me a different story:

My mama is very ill. She would visit me or pick me up, but she is too sick with tuberculosis. She tried to visit me, but they won't let her in. I could run away, I guess. I have before, but I didn't go home then. I looked for my friend.

Running away from homes is common among children in orphanages and boarding homes. Staff at the home in Pushkin lament this fact but add:

We almost always find them again. You see, even though we only have one person per 300 children on call at night, we prevent running away by locking up their shoes at night in a closet. That way, in the winter they don't go far or the police knows where they belong when they encounter them at the Pushkin railway station.

Even with the locking up of shoes at night, a few do run away.

For children at a boarding home or orphanage, life is about beating the system, getting away with things, and not getting caught breaking rules. By around the age of eight, children like Masha do not strive to learn anything at school or to be "good." Their goal is self-satisfaction and survival. These children do not aim to please others because in the end, doing as adults will is not apparently beneficial. Following rules at a boarding home results in fewer or even no personal possessions, less freedom, and a minimal existence. Fighting the system however, yields material possessions, possibly money, and even some treats, like a visit to McDonald's from time to time.

Beating the system is not, however, only a street child or orphan way of life. Rather, it is part of the Russian way of life. Already in school, children are tempted to outsmart and rebel against the regulations of teachers, who impose a rigid discipline in the classroom. In the average and typical Russian school, children are expected to sit quietly at their desks and raise their hand while keeping their elbows on the desk. Traditionally, when called upon, children must stand to answer. Children will generally comply when it comes to classroom decorum. During tests, however, cheating is common. From answers on small papers to lists written on legs under skirts, children are most creative.

Upon finishing school, those who wish to enter the university are faced with another challenge: getting in. First and foremost, grades must meet a minimum. Most children have tutors to help them prepare for the entrance exams and many tutors directly involved in the examination process are paid off to pass the students. Young adults also pay the military so as not to serve or continue to pay tuition to a college or institute so as to avoid military duty. Payoffs are part of getting by in Russia.

Payoffs often go hand in hand with another ingredient for survival in Russia: *blat*. Roughly defined, *blat* is influence or pull and depends on credit you may have, either in money or in kind, with another person. The *blat* system relies on the relationships a family or individual develops over time. These relationships may include acquaintances at work, friends, and relatives, as well as one's friends' or acquaintances' relatives, friends, and acquaintances. Moreover, the quality and possibly the length of the list may add to one's ability to acquire more power and ability to manipulate the *blat* system. Pesmen writes, " 'Shifty' behavior and shameless name-dropping were, in part, also the Russian exposing some of the special capital he commanded in his 'system.' "[16] On a daily basis, the average Russian may use *blat* to obtain very basic items of food and clothing. It is a system that appears to Russians as invaluable, not even corrupt, in order to get by during social and economic chaos.

An orphan's desire to maximize her ability to survive and to reap as many benefits as possible is reinforced by the adult world that surrounds her. While patience and suffering are accepted as fate by most Russians, beating the system a little bit every day is also part of the Russian way.

CULTURAL CONSTRAINTS IN HELPING HOMELESS CHILDREN IN RUSSIA: NOTIONS OF *SVOI*, *CHUZHOI*, AND VICTIMHOOD

Questions remain as to why a society that traditionally idealizes childhood is finding it difficult to understand and save the children most in need. Part of the answer lies in the economic difficulties Russia faces today. However, from an anthropological perspective, the problem runs on a sociocultural level. In interviews, adults with various educational backgrounds discussed the feelings they have when approaching orphans. Some cannot bear to face the children, so overcome are they by emotion. Others fear these children to be dishonest and potential criminals. Yet others feel they need to care for themselves and their children first and do not have time, money, or energy to commit to orphans who, in their words, cannot truly be helped anyway. The pervasive inability or unwillingness to face other people's problems is due not only to a lack of financial stability, but also to a pervasive feeling among Russians that they are unable to make a change in society.

These feelings and attitudes have developed over time, a result of enculturation and socialization. Negative sentiments toward street children are the outcome of a complex web of teachings under the Soviet regime, a stigma placed on that which is different, foreign, and "not one's own," and a cultural-religious sense of martyrdom.

In the past, the average Russian citizen has been discouraged from proactive engagement in social issues. Under the Soviet regime, becoming involved in social problems only disclosed the fact that they existed. Instead, orphans and children with disabilities were confined to institutions. Indeed, many of the adults interviewed were convinced that under the Soviet regime, orphans and disabled children barely existed. Since the collapse of the Soviet regime, Russians have not been given much reason to believe that their vote counts. Instead, they once again feel victimized by the socioeconomic crisis and helpless in the face of social and political turmoil. Even with money and an education in hand, few feel they have the power to make a difference in society.

"Why do Americans want to adopt our children?" is a question I often encounter while studying orphans in Russia. Before I even begin to answer this question, the person will probably add, "Most of our orphans have all kinds of physical and psychological problems! And why do Americans want a child that is not theirs, neither by birth nor by nationality?" When asked whether they would ever consider adopting, a common response is, "Perhaps if there was no way I could have my own. But even then, I would have to think about it. One's own is always better."

One's own: *Svoi*. A value-laden concept that underlies not only day-to-day individual and family decisions, but social and political trends as well. Not one's own, *ne svoi*, will never understand and feel the way *svoi* would.

Ne svoi is closely related to *chuzhoi*, which means strange or foreign. Many Russians feel they can never really integrate foreign blood into their society. From a Russian's perspective, one who is *chuzhoi* will never fully become Russian, even if that person was born and raised on Russian soil. It is in their blood to be different, just like orphans have it in their blood to be different.

Russian adults approach orphans with trepidation since such children remain stigmatized. To this day, adults interviewed agree that an orphan potentially has bad genes and is a threat to society. The argument frequently made is that the parents of these children were incapable of raising the children and therefore the children are likely to have inherited these negative qualities. As under the Soviet regime, adults today are afraid to adopt. Those who do often do not tell anyone that their children are adopted, including the children themselves.

This is not to deny the fact that many of the orphans have physical or emotional problems. Indeed, fetal alcohol syndrome, for example, continues to plague many of the children forced into orphanages. However, as many adoptions in the West have demonstrated, it is frequently the absence of a stable family life, love, and opportunities to succeed, and not genetic makeup, that force the children to become social outcasts.

Of course, exceptions are made. Being different may sometimes be better. Sergei, a doctoral candidate in Russian literature and a strong believer in the strength of Russian culture, tells of an orphan who was different, but truly special:

He was adopted by my relatives. We all knew, but of course no one ever told him. He grew up in our dark-haired family and his blond hair and blue eyes were a striking contrast. He was like an angel, both in looks and in character: such a good person. Then, just as he entered his youth, he was shot. As if he was not meant long for this human world.

Even in the situation where an adopted child is loved and appreciated, the difference, the *ne svoi,* is still pointed out.

Another hindrance to helping homeless children and orphans comes from a sense of continuous hardship and martyrdom. *"Kakaya nasha zhizn' tyazhiolaya"* or "How hard life is" is a phrase heard every day in homes, casual conversation, and even in public spaces. Even when life seems to be going particularly well, for example, if one just bought a new apartment, was given a well-paying job, and received a tourist visa to the United States (as was the case with one of my Russian acquaintances), one might still begin the day with a deep sigh and proclaim, *"Kakaya nasha zhizn' tyazhiolaya!"*

Sergei adds that Russians and Americans simply do not view life the same way: "The difference between Americans and Russians is that an American may walk by a beggar, think, 'Indeed, how sad. How hard life is,' and walk on, sparing perhaps a kopek or two. The thought of truly helping this person never occurs [to a Russian]." Most Russians, according to many interviewed, do not feel they have any power to help. Life is too overwhelming, complicated, and oppressive. For those who have the financial means to help, the issues do not appear as important to the country. One businessman, upon my arrival in Russia and questioning him about the homeless situation responded, "Homeless children? We don't have them anymore."

CONCLUSION

The divide in worldview between Russian adults with homes and Russian homeless children is immense. Each understands childhood in different terms: The adult sees childhood as a protected and nurtured time of life, while the homeless child sees childhood as a time of independent struggle with the demands of the adult world. Adults see homeless children as victims of the evils of their society, yet also as untouchables; homeless children see themselves as manipulators of a world they mistrust. Unlike those trying to save the children from the streets, these children themselves believe they cannot be helped. Stoecker cites:

Answering questions about their dreams and desires, homeless children in 1999 do not want, as they did before, nice clothing, toys, books. They do not hope to be adopted and do not want help with finding homes. Today's homeless are tougher, less trustful and more pessimistic.[17]

Homeless children, in a sense, are at war with the adult world in which they live. The adults, whether from Western charity organizations or hired by the Russian government, nurture this war by rounding up homeless children and trying to force them to grow up in prisonlike institutions. This war will be lost on both ends if adults do not take the initiative, as they have in past wars, to "understand the enemy." Homeless children need to be understood and taken care of beyond their physical requirements. They need to be respected differently from children who have been nurtured in families. They need to be seen as extremely able and empowered by their experiences while simultaneously being marginalized by the world in which they exist.

It is my hope that via an anthropological contextualization of the reality orphans face on a daily basis, those reaching out to homeless children will come together and touch these children on a deeper level than in the past, thus ending the rift that exists between the Russian adult and homeless children's worlds.

Chapter 5

The Lure of the City

In the world of poverty-stricken children there exists an overarching myth: that life in the big city is a step up from rural life, that in the city, a child is free, that work in the city will pay for a "normal" life. At first glance, life in the city for the impoverished child seems to hold more promise than life in the countryside. After all, only in a city may the poor interact with the rich, possibly earning a salary of some kind and finding shelter in public spaces. Life in the countryside, however, may lead to starvation: In Russia, for example, products are frequently not delivered and salaries are not regular, with families going for months without wages.

Poor and abandoned children find the city alluring. Russian children, for example, see Moscow as modern and technologically advanced, as a center of progress and opportunity. In fact, approximately 98 percent of the street children in Moscow are from surrounding provinces.[1] It has been noted by scholars of developing countries that cities "attract migrants with their glitter and liveliness,"[2] which mask the harsh reality the poor face. For just as there is this aspect of progress and advancement in cities, so there is the side of violence, subversion, abuse, drugs, prostitution, crime, and exposure to extreme health hazards. The urban environment presents many obstacles that are at times insurmountable for the abandoned child. These include problems of resource distribution, exploitation, disease, and, from a cultural perspective, discrimination and stigmatization. In short, while the city offers hope for the destitute, it also threatens their slow demise in sundry ways.

To date, street children and their urban environments are still rarely studied. Some of the most popular countries researched on the subject of street children and juvenile delinquency include Brazil, the Philippines, Kenya, and India. These have come to the world's attention due to the high rate of childhood poverty, abuse, and violence. However, countries in which the incidence of child abandonment and homelessness is still merely rising (albeit at staggering rates) are often ignored or merely given lip service. The problem is explained as not problematic enough in relation to other economic or social problems a given nation faces. The fact that children help to mold the dominant culture, that they are active participants in and creators of the urban landscape in which they live, is left ignored. The social chaos in which they survive is also shaped by their own subculture, and so a vicious cycle begins. Because the topic of youth and city culture has few supporters, the city, which on the one hand appears so alluring and fantastic, is also home to many a child's emotional and physical death.

When homes offer little stability, or in times of family crises, or when emotional problems prevail, many teens both at home and abroad feel compelled to run away. In the United States, approximately 60 percent of runaways have parents who abuse alcohol and/or drugs. Seventy percent have used narcotics themselves. Fifty percent of runaway children have experienced abuse at home. Eighty percent of runaway children have serious behavioral or emotional problems.[3] It can be assumed that if any of these factors are present in a home, a child is predisposed to running away. According to a recent study, "family dysfunction, parental neglect, family drug use and implications of sexual activity by the runaway are seen as strong indicators of running away by youth."[4] These factors have reached extreme heights in many developing countries, and it is not surprising then that the number of street children is rising at a critical rate. An abusive, unhealthy home environment, juxtaposed with the mythic promises of the urban dream, leads many children to migrate to the city streets to try their fortune or fate.

Russian cities are prime sites for the coexistence of such urban dichotomies. Throughout the Soviet regime, urbanization involved the development of both social progress and decay. During the Soviet era, urbanization was a trend, with the highest rates of growth occurring in the 1950s when migration from rural areas accounted for 60 percent of urban growth.[5] Throughout Russian history, the city has been depicted as perhaps the only place where one may find higher education, scientific development, better communication systems, and fine art—in short, what is considered "civilization." Cultured people (*kul'turnye liudi*) are not considered to be easily found in the countryside and many urbanites to this day will distinguish between those who have a long family tradition in the city and those whose origins may be found in rural areas. However, amid this wealth of high culture, urban growth has also fueled growth in complexity and heterogeneity, for the development of "microworlds and microsocieties," for the emergence of youth subcultures,[6] and for the spread of non-elite groups such as homeless people and street children.

Lawlessness is one characteristic of the Russian urban landscape that impacts social psychology and the formation and viability of many of Russia's subcultures. While throughout Soviet history the official government remained deaf to the demands of the people, profiting from the disadvantaged and powerless, youth groups developed underground systems to satisfy the cultural needs of its members. As Bushnell and other scholars have documented, "there was a complex network of art exhibits, plays, poetry readings, and other unofficial but nevertheless frequent and widespread cultural performances."[7] As more information from the West came in, curiosity of the general public rose and various informal groups created their own means to meet the demands of the public. Corruption and bribery became an acceptable means to achieve otherwise legitimate goals censured by those in power. To this day, corruption and illegitimacy are accepted and are the norm in Russia.

Distinguishing between necessary and criminal is often difficult and it comes as no surprise then that the average child, much less a desperate child trying to survive on the streets of Moscow, might not differentiate between right and wrong the same way we might in the United States. Poor children continue to flock to urban streets for they offer "opportunities" to succeed in life through petty theft and hooliganism, opportunities that "eclipse anything the countryside could offer."[8]

This chapter seeks to illuminate various myths that guide abandoned children throughout the world, but particularly in Russia, to choose life on the city streets. Their decision to do so immediately makes them victims of invisible yet real threats to their health and well-being, such as pollution and disease. Lack of adult aid to these children is a result only in part of poor economic and political systems. It is also a result of cultural issues, including lack of understanding of the children's perspectives. This, in turn, is a result of historical cultural taboos against street children, that blind the adult world to the true potential and reality of each individual abandoned child. In the conclusion of this overview, I will propose four main ingredients to a successful urban youth aid program. These ingredients are often assumed to be included by NGOs and donor agencies, but in fact they are only infrequently present abroad.

THE MYTH OF THE URBAN ENVIRONMENT

Children in developing rural areas often complain of the harshness of their environment: extreme temperatures, lack of plumbing and electricity, poor access to food, and other material disparities, real or imagined, compared to city life. Cities promise, if not less severe climates with high-rise buildings screening some of the harsher winds in the winter or emitting warmth, for example, plumbing, electricity, and access to jobs. However, from an environmental perspective, the urban environment is fraught with air, water, and land pollution. In a number of Russian cities industrial pollution persists. Households also contribute to air pollution, with environmentally unfriendly means of heating and automobile usage. Landfills, unsanitary means of garbage, and waste disposal contribute to the spread of toxins in the air and water, as well as to the multiplication of vermin. Approximately eighty-four Russian cities have air pollution ten times in excess of the Russian Federation's allowable concentrations.[9]

Children, generally more active than adults, are more likely to inhale more of the polluted air relative to their body weight. Playing in the ground exposes them to polluted soil. Children working the streets are most exposed to these pollutants because they wash with and may even drink toxic water and are surrounded by exhaust fumes and other pollutants. In St. Petersburg, children pride themselves on not getting sick from drinking the notorious bad water and will flaunt their immunity by drinking it for an audience. Long-term effects remain uncertain. Children are less aware of these health hazards and, in effect, are even more likely to be exposed to them.

Statistics indicate that in developing urban evironments, children are more likely to become ill from pollution:

Infants and children in developing countries are several hundred times more likely to die from diarrhea, pneumonia and measles than are children in Europe or North America. . . . When they do not die, children living in such extremely polluted environments may grow up stunted and handicapped. . . . A definite increase in the incidence of cancer and allergy symptoms has also been detected in urban areas of industrialized countries, due to air pollution from industrial emissions, vehicle exhausts, tobacco smoke and chemicals from building materials combined with poor ventilation. These factors have been connected with the increase in cases of asthma in large cities.[10]

Pollution causes 20 percent of Russian children to be born with deformities or defects.[11] Studies have shown an increase in respiratory and gastrointestinal illnesses as being linked in part to environmental pollution. Interfax reported in March 2001 that 70 percent of Russian young people aged ten to fifteen now suffer from chronic diseases.

THE MYTH OF SHELTER IN CITIES

In Russia life in the countryside is harsh. With temperatures plummeting well below freezing in the winter, the poorly insulated shacks of many poor rural dwellers, lacking in basic amenities such as running water and electricity, seem hardly appropriate. In fact, the daily strategy to stay warm and survive in rural Russia is so tedious that the warm public train stations offer a better housing situation for many children. As is the Russian custom to spend summers in the countryside and winters in the city, so, too, do many street urchins, returning to their home villages in the summer. However, public spaces can barely suffice as shelter for the developing child, even if only seasonally.

Children are known to live below the platforms of railway stations in Moscow and St. Petersburg. Besides dirt, general physical discomfort, and other obvious problems with such shelter, these children face roundups by police with tear gas attacks. Other shelters of choice include pipes, parked buses, and commuter trains. Few of the children live in one of the two official shelters in Moscow. By age sixteen or seventeen, many die due to sickness and malnutrition, and many simply freeze to death. Nonetheless, few of the children want to be helped by shelters. They feel they are better off without the aid of an adult. In a letter to President Vladimir Putin, homeless children wrote:

If you want to help us, give us money. We will dress well and go to McDonald's. At the moment they throw us out, telling us we are dirty. . . . We won't go to orphanages willingly, because there they will want to educate us and we can survive on our own, without grown-ups.[12]

With nowhere to turn for help, street children have lost faith in adults, and their newly found child society feels more like home, providing more security and warmth than the "home" they left.

THE MYTH OF DISEASE

Most children entering life on the streets are convinced that they will not be affected by the many diseases plaguing the country. To some extent, they may feel invincible. On another level, they do not imagine that they will take on jobs or lifestyles that will expose them to such viruses as AIDS or tuberculosis. Moreover, they have heard that hospitals are everywhere in the city, unlike in the countryside. Help is surely always just a few blocks away.

However, urban environments in developing countries offer little help to the underpaid, unfed, and uneducated children who fall victim to its allure and who are also lacking a sense of values and tradition. As rigid social control in many developing countries, including Russia, fluctuates, old values and norms are tested and new ones remain undeveloped. Children living on city streets have little direction, no sense of the future, and, thus, little to strive for besides their daily needs being met. Prostitutes on the streets of urban Russia, for example, are fully aware of the threat of AIDS and the means to protect themselves, but they will, for extra pay, work without protection.

In the United States, most runaway children turn to prostitution to survive.[13] Similarly, homeless children in developing countries sell their bodies for bread and shelter. Many independently walk the streets while others become sexual slaves. Disease is almost inevitable.

Weakened by hunger, disease, drug use, parasites, and lack of shelter, street children encounter a vicious cycle: They are pushed deeper into desperation as they are less able to fend for themselves. Many of the street children are victims of the HIV/AIDS epidemic, orphaned because their parents suffered from the virus, and, because of the lack of social and medical support, they find themselves poorer and weaker. According to facts published by UNAIDS, HIV/AIDS affects all developing countries in similar ways:

- AIDS pushes people deeper into poverty as households lose their breadwinners, livelihoods are compromised, and savings are consumed by the cost of health care and funerals.
- Women are almost invariably left bearing even bigger burdens—as workers, caregivers, educators and mothers. At the same time, their legal, social, and political status often leaves them more vulnerable to HIV/AIDS.
- The HIV/AIDS epidemic is putting the health sector under more strain.
- The epidemic is reducing the overall quality of care provided. A shortage of hospital beds, for example, means that people tend to be admitted only in the latter stages of illness, which reduces their chances of recovery.
- The vast majority of people living with HIV/AIDS worldwide are in the prime of their working lives.
- AIDS weakens economic activity by squeezing productivity, adding cost, diverting productive resources, and depleting skills.[14]

The number of HIV/AIDS cases has continued to grow in Eastern Europe since the 1990s at an alarming rate. It has been called an explosion by such scholars as the UNAIDS Director Dr. Peter Piot.[15] According to the 2002 UNAIDS fact sheet, approximately 1 million people in Eastern Europe and Central Asia are living with HIV/AIDS, twice the number at the end of 1999. Of the Eastern European countries, Russia is leading the surge in HIV cases. New cases are doubling annually. Statistics show that:

The vast majority of HIV infections are among young people—chiefly those who inject drugs. It is estimated that up to 1% of the population of countries in the Commonwealth of Independent States is injecting drugs, placing these people and their sexual partners at high risk of infection.[16]

The data on drug use, however, does not underscore the significant rise in sexually transmitted HIV cases. More women are contracting HIV through sexual transmission and "more pregnant women are testing positive for HIV—suggesting a shift of the epidemic into the wider population."[17] Young people, especially those living outside the home, are becoming active sexually at earlier ages.

A rise in cases of sexually transmitted diseases in general has been overwhelming to health services already noted for their inefficiency and chaotic state. In 1995, Russia had the highest number of reported syphilis cases seen last century.[18] The explosion has been superficially fueled by an increase in drug abuse and lack of blood screening and prevention programs. Underlying the epidemic, however, is an unwillingness of Eastern European society to acknowledge and confront the problem.

The explosion has left no one safe. Everyone is at risk. Unsterilized needles are still common, so anyone needing a shot is vulnerable. In Romania, for example:

In 1995 more than 90 percent of the cases were among children, most of whom, it was suspected, were infected by contaminated needles and syringes. At that time, the country had more than half of Europe's juvenile cases of HIV infection and AIDS. . . . In the Russian Federation, 277 children were registered as HIV-positive in 1995; 94 of them had AIDS. By September 1997, some 3,000 new HIV cases in children were registered for that year, a number many health officials say reflects underreporting. In general, infection rates are underreported and reliable figures are hard to obtain.[19]

According to the majority of the reports analyzed for this discussion, the estimated number of people now living with HIV in the Russian

Federation is considered four times higher than the claimed numbers.[20] What is important in the data is not merely the figures but the phenomenon of underreporting. Underreporting, like so many factors leading to the health crisis in Eastern Europe, represents the tendency to ignore or even deny, much less act upon, social issues that in some way clash with cultural norms. And it is not just AIDS that is considered a social taboo. Simple preventative measures are also seen as an embarrassment, including condom use and sex education courses. Other problems that remain unaddressed include incest, rape, prostitution, and sexually transmitted diseases. Marginalized groups, such as homosexuals, find little basis for self-expression and inclusion in society and are left to their own devises when combating the stigmatized infection, finding medication only rarely and by unofficial means. Only the Czech Republic and Georgia have included these topics in school curricula.[21]

Besides the HIV/AIDS crisis, tuberculosis exists as an invisible threat to Russian street children. Once again, even with underreporting of incidences, the numbers are staggering. According to one report, the country is averaging 150,000 new cases annually.[22] The most extreme outbreaks occur in prisons, where medicine is distributed randomly and incompletely, creating drug-resistant strains of the disease. Unfortunately, many street children are being placed in prisons with adults, as there is a lack of juvenile detention facilities. In fact, many street children are simply held in prisons until they are officially placed in shelters or orphanages. Because of the cultural taboo against certain health issues, the Russian public remains ignorant of the crisis and of the effect it could have on all. For instance, many are convinced that AIDS is only significant to the lives of homosexuals and drug users.

Finally, there remains an overwhelming feeling of helplessness among Russians. As the numbers begin to be published, Russians generally shrug it off as yet another problem beyond their realm of influence. From the street child to the educated adult, the belief is that if you are not directly in power and rich, your voice gets lost. Lena, a former prostitute and drug user, comments on HIV, "We can't cope with it on our own,"[23] and a mother and editor explains, "I take care of my own; that is all I can do."[24]

This feeling of helplessness is part of a larger Russian cultural sentiment of ambivalence, fatalism, and even victimization. At a gathering, in response to American businessmen complaining that Russians simply do not seem to care about helping their society develop economically, Elena F., an actress from St. Petersburg, replied, "It's not that we don't care, but when it comes to making a difference, Russians are ambivalent or fatalistic. Our approach to life is guided by the maxim of *avos'*." When asked to define the term *avos'*, Elena said that she could only describe it by way of an example. "Russians don't worry about whether or not a certain number of people will fit into an elevator, they simply step in and wait to find out." Not just Elena, but scholars of Russia since the nineteenth century have commented on this notion of *avos'*. Scholars have gone further to link *avos'* to Russians' lack of sense of cultural identity and have faulted Russians for taking on other nations' identities in search of their own. *Avos'* is linked to a feeling of victimization, or even "victimhood," as an inevitable experience of Russian life that entails the experience of *terpenie* (patience) and *stradanie* (suffering), hindering Russian social progress and development on the one hand, yet, on the other, evoking a sense of communitas and, in effect, liberating the individual in times of economic and political turmoil.

Beyond the feeling of powerlessness is the aftermath of Soviet control: fear that getting involved could hurt the individual and her or his family. If you speak up, you get noticed and people will try to stop you by whatever means they have. In Russia, that means the mafia may be after you, or so those interviewed insinuated.

DISPELLING THE MYTHS

In general, targeting populations through education programs before an epidemic such as HIV/AIDS takes place could be one way to prevent social and biological diseases, if the education is sensitive to its population. A few successful programs have been documented in both Brazil and Russia. "Brazil's widely praised efforts to provide universal treatment and care, in addition to its well-planned prevention programs, are estimated to have avoided 234,000 hospitalizations in 1996–2000."[25] Such education programs are often designed by individual communities, since little help is given from the outside on which to model their programs.

Relatively small endeavors of opening clinics to help victims of stigmatized health issues have been proven to be effective even in Russia. In the Saratov region, the local government helped fund one such clinic. While initially in 1998 only 400 people came for HIV testing, in 2002, 10,000 appeared.[26] One of only two rehabilitation centers for heroin addicts in Irkutsk boasts a 50 percent success rate.[27] The success of these programs rests on their emergence from a deep understanding of the scarcity, neglect, and discrimination[28] the targeted population experiences.

Although developers and politicians independently may attempt to aid urban youth in distress throughout the world, they are often too removed from the youth they are trying to help. Programs have been initiated by foreigners, for example, leading to misappropriation and outright theft of funding and little contact with those the programs were designed to help in the first place. Such programs are often short lived, leading to even more disillusionment among the needy. Naïve goodwill may fail and even alienate the very population it is trying to help.

There are four ingredients essential for a program to succeed. First, it must be organized by minds that understand the day-to-day lives of the subjects, their conditions and their potential. Such individuals would understand best what the subjects experience, and further, the social and legal context. Outside officials cannot affect and interact with the local population successfully if they do not share the same experiences. It is important to be sensitive to the cultural relativity of children's lives in every country and community. While we can confidently say that certain factors, such as domestic violence, impoverishment, and familial substance abuse, raise the likelihood worldwide of children to end up on the streets, other factors are culturally dependent. Whereas in the United States the absence of one parent has been identified as a contributing factor to why teenagers run away, it has not been determined to influence a child's decision in Russia on any large scale.[29] In Russia, the absence of a father is extremely common and seen by many children interviewed as "normal."

Second, a successful program must offer continuity in support and indispensable services.[30] Mentorship programs and medical facilities need to persist after rehabilitation. Often the mere presence of these programs beyond individual rehabilitation serves as a security blanket and motivates "survivors" to persist.

Third, a successful programs needs to target not just the street children themselves, but the culture and community surrounding such youth, for, as Blanc confirms:

It is obvious that the existence of the child and the conditions of existence are totally dependent on what the child means to us. If a child is regarded as expendable—even if an asset—care will be inadequate. This will be reflected not only in high infant mortality rates, but also, in other health, education and social indicators, such as the high incidence among children of preventable disease, high dropout rates and high institutionalization rates for juvenile offenders.[31]

While on the one hand, the adult world heralds the child, idealizes it, and cherishes it in individual instances and philosophically, in most urban landscapes today, the street child does not reap the benefits of this ideal. This is reflected in the increasing numbers of abandoned, abused, and neglected street children. The conditions of life for the average street child parallel the value placed on the abandoned child.

A fourth ingredient characteristic of a successful program is a high rate of interaction with other programs. Too often, especially in Russia, organizations will work to improve conditions for a select group of individuals. They work independently and are isolated from other similar programs and rarely communicate with those bureaucracies concerned with children's problems. In Russia, nine different official agencies are charged with dealing with the problem of street children (these include the Education Ministry, Labor Ministry, and Interior Ministry), leading to none of them dealing successfully. A joke one former street child brings up: "There are two ways to deal with a problem: One is to do something, and the other is to form a committee."

Chapter 6

Domestic Violence Contributing to Child Homelessness

Tatyana Sudakova and Sally W. Stoecker

A WORD ABOUT THE RESEARCH COLLABORATION

With funding from the American Council on Teachers of Russian (ACTR) and the Transnational Crime and Corruption Center (TraCCC) at American University, Sally Stoecker spent the summer of 2000 researching the problem of child homelessness and exploitation in Irkutsk, Russia. She was affiliated with the criminology department of Baikal State University and Economics and Law. Professors Anna Repetskaya and Viola Rybal'skaya assigned their colleague, Tatyana Sudakova, to work with Sally to arrange meetings with practitioners, locate sources, and help with interviews and translations. Through this collaboration grew common research interests and friendship. Tatyana Sudakova recently defended her thesis on the criminological characteristics of criminal behavior among minors who use drugs and is now Candidate of Science at Baikal State University where she teaches courses in criminology and criminal law. Tatyana and Sally plan to continue their collaboration in the areas of homelessness and juvenile crime and to publicize the plight of children in Russia and United States.

INTRODUCTION

Crimes against children and child homelessness are phenomena that have reached epidemic proportions in Russia. According to the Russian Procuracy, crimes against children have grown more brutal in recent years, despite a downturn in registered crimes.[1] Last year, 94,000 children were injured or killed. The Center for the Promotion of Criminal Justice in Moscow reports that increasingly, murders are made to look like accidents and in many, if not most, cases are committed by the child's parents. Infanticide and rape are becoming more common, as is the criminal exploitation of homeless children. In this chapter, we will examine why crimes against children, especially those committed by parents and guardians, are increasing and how this is feeding and perpetuating the problem of child homelessness in Russia.

Today in Russia there are about 36 million youth.[2] Every year the number of children in the Russian Federation declines precipitously. Official statistics show that this number has declined by 4 million in the past five years. The Committee of State Statistics estimates that it will fall to 25 million by 2005. One of the reasons for this gloomy demographic trend is that the rights of children to a safe and wholesome childhood are constantly being violated. In an attempt to protect themselves from regular family abuse, nearly 2,000 minors commit suicide and 30,000 leave home and in effect become homeless. Running away from home and thereby sparing themselves abuse by those persons closest to them, minors become "street children." Many street children in turn become predisposed to criminal behavior and heightened *victimnost'*—that is, the characteristics and qualities that give rise to the likelihood that they will become victims of crimes committed against them by other persons.

Homelessness has really overwhelmed Russia, just as it did after the Bolshevik Revolution in the 1920s and World War II in the mid- to late 1940s. The enormous loss of life in the upheavals of revolution, war, and famine left thousands, if not millions, of dislocated children without parents or guardians. With nowhere to turn, the children naturally turned to the streets and begged for alms or stole food.[3] Child homelessness in Russia today is especially tragic because unlike the postwar period, most of the children classified as orphans have parents who are alive. According to Russian Deputy Prime Minister Valentina Matviyenko, 80 percent of the 1 million homeless children[4] living in Russia have parents or guardians.[5] Parental neglect, due to the physical and psychological incapacities of the parents and/or guardians or the burdens associated with current unemployment trends that require single mothers to work several jobs simultaneously in order to support their children, lay at the core of today's homeless epidemic. In addition, the demise of *vseobuch* or "education for all" in Russia, where fewer children are attending school and are spending time on the streets. According to the Ministry of Education in Russia, 367,696 children between the ages of five and seventeen did not attend school in 2000.

In 1990, the Russian Supreme Soviet ratified the United Nations' Convention on the Rights of the Child and presidential decrees were issued to back it up. In the mid-1990s, spurred on by the unprecedented growth of child homelessness, a group of scholars and practitioners developed a policy on homelessness and juvenile crime that became the foundation for the law adopted by the Federal Assembly in June 1999 on preventing homelessness and juvenile crime. According to juvenile crime experts, the law is especially important in legalizing the protection of children's rights at the federal level and making these rights the basis of preventative work for the first time in Russian legal history. The new law, however, has many deficiencies because it fails to create a system for enacting the new law. As deputy chairperson of the Duma committee on legislation, Elena Mizulina, puts it:

This is typical of our legislation. We announce attractive and timely reforms but do not create a system or work out a mechanism that would allow the reforms to be realized. That is why the effectiveness of the law is so weak.[6]

While this is an important first step, laws to control family violence have yet to be adopted—other than rape or assault—at the federal level. Family abuse and child homelessness are multifaceted phenomena that are based on considerable research among sociologists, criminologists, and medical professionals. From a criminological perspective, we suggest that child homelessness is related to the role of violence within the family. A child's exposure to domestic violence, whether leveled at the child directly or at other family members, may influence a child's decision to leave home and live on the street. However, it is extremely difficult to establish a direct link between these two phenomena, especially because violence in the family is usually concealed out of shame. We can only skim the surface of the problem by examining the statistics in the Ministry of Internal Affairs (MVD) reports of cruelty toward children or cases whereby the health and well-being of children were violated to various degrees. This includes cases of murder in which the victims are the children and the perpetrators are their parents (natural or adoptive) or legal guardians. Another reason that linkages are hard to establish is that children and youth are not emotionally mature enough to differentiate between appropriate and inappropriate behavior. Because they do not know their elementary rights or how to seek protection, in many cases children view neglectful and even criminal behavior as "normal."

DEFINITIONS/TERMINOLOGY

In order to discuss the linkages between abuse and homelessness, it is imperative to provide definitions of the phenomena under discussion, taking into account both the Russian and Western contexts and usages.

What Is a Child?

For the purposes of this discussion, we use the common understanding (in Russian civil law and American jurisprudence) of a child (also referred to as "youth" or "minor") as a person who has not reached eighteen years of age. In most cases, we will refer to a child as a victim of abuse; however, in instances where we discuss a juvenile *offender*, a child is defined as a person between the ages of fourteen to eighteen. In Russia, a child can be held responsible for committing a crime only if she or he is fourteen years of age or older. In the United States, the age of criminal responsibility varies from state to state and on the nature of a given case (especially murder). There have been instances where children as young as seven have been held responsible for their crimes.

Domestic Violence

The term "domestic violence" or "domestic abuse" in the West is often used to describe abuse inflicted by or against one's spouse or intimate partner and does not usually connote abuse of children or minors. Family violence in the legal sense has broader application in that it covers not only spousal abuse, but abuse between parents and children as well. It also refers to situations in which children witness violence between their parents.[7] In Russian literature, the term for domestic abuse (*domashnee nasiliye*) draws on its very root—"home" (*dom*). However, this choice of wording is also problematic as it connotes a narrow view of the problem, confining it to behavior within the home when such abuse can occur in other locations. Although both terms, domestic and family, indicate familial or relational ties among family members, it is also important to have a broad understanding of the term "family member" because in many cases children reside with persons who are not blood relatives. "Child abuse" is clearly a strong candidate for use in this work, but we want to recognize that the abuse, especially psychological, can result from children witnessing violence between other family members that may not be directed at the child. Therefore, for the purposes of this chapter, we will employ the term "family abuse" in order to have a broader understanding of the problem than that associated with child abuse and domestic violence.

Abusive behavior against children and youth should be understood as action or threat of action that is characterized by physical, psychological, sexual, or emotional abuse against a victim affecting her or his life, health, or sexuality that violates criminal law. In the broadest sense, abuse can be defined as behavior that causes harm to others and limits free choice—"usurps free will."[8] From the perspective of criminal law and criminology, the term "family abuse" with respect to minors can be broken down into at least four forms:[9]

1. *Physical abuse*: actions against a minor that cause physical pain and suffering.
2. *Psychological abuse*: actions against a minor that cause psychological suffering or a high degree of psychic tension.
3. *Sexual abuse*: violation of a minor's sexual inviolability, accompanied by physical and/or psychological suffering.
4. *Emotional abuse*: actions against a minor that cause emotional stress.

Physical Abuse

Although the idea of physical violence may seem straightforward, it is multifaceted and complex. How do we classify spankings, slapping, and other forms of corporal punishment—actions that combine elements of both physical and psychological abuse? Although the child may accept this as the norm, she may also experience considerable stress because corporal punishment is a serious humiliation. Periodic spankings can be a source of maladjustment. Corporal punishment is always a form degradation and it not only contributes to a child's fear, but it also teaches a child improper behavior toward others.

Psychological Abuse

Psychological abuse takes two forms: verbal and nonverbal. Verbal abuse involves threatening statements, humiliation, degradation, and so on. Nonverbal abuse involves threatening actions, such as the perpetrator threatening the child with a knife, and often becomes a combination of physical and psychological abuse. The psychological literature describes child abuse as a type of child rearing referred to in Russian as "hedgehog gloves" (*yezhovyie rukavitsy*). An extreme example is raising a child in an environment devoid of compassion and respect. Rather, the environment is one of heated aggression filled with hatred and sadistic relations as well as the regular infliction of physical force and/or denial of food and water for several days at a time. The psychological profile and social status of the child are important. Because children are dependent on their parents materially and psychologically, they do not complain about abuse but rather prefer to leave home. The fact that they are unaware of their elementary rights complicates the situation. Moreover, mother-child ties are very important to boys and girls, therefore it is not surprising that despite any kind treatment by strangers, a child is drawn closer to the mother, regardless of how poorly she acts and how indifferently she relates to her child.

Emotional Abuse

Closely related to psychological abuse is emotional abuse. The child is not critical of her parents because that is all she knows. The child develops a stereotype of parental behavior. She may feel sorry for her mother because she loves her. In this kind of contradictory situation, a child may become afflicted with post-traumatic stress. Emotional abuse can affect the health and psychological state of the victim just as much as physical abuse does.

Cruel, Degrading, and Inhumane Treatment

The concept of cruelty against children varies among cultures and societies. The "Declaration on Neglect of Parental Duty and Maltreatment of Children," adopted at the 36th World Medical Assembly in Singapore in 1984, related "maltreatment" to physical, sexual, or emotional cruelty as well as negligence of parental duty—inability or failure of parents or guardians to provide for the child's basic needs and adequate level of care. "Neglect" is defined as failure to fulfill responsibilities, such as ensuring that the child is fed properly, clothed, given medical check-ups and treatment, and protected from actions that threaten the child's physical and psychological well-being.

Today, specialists speak of a "syndrome" of child maltreatment in the family because the instances of physical abuse are not isolated but are unrelenting. In fact, it has almost become a trend that is manifested in various ways—including physical and/or sexual abuse, neglect of child-rearing obligations, and maltreatment in the form of emotional abuse.

Families of Misfortune/State of the Family

The contemporary family—as an important microcosm of society, charged with performing child-raising functions—is faced with an assortment of problems. In many cases, families are run and children are raised by single parents or other relatives, such as the grandmother. In many cases, this is accompanied by amoral parental or guardian behavior and psychological dysfunction in the family. These are the most commonplace forms of family misfortune. The pathology of family relations, first of all, affects various aspects of deviation in a child's behavior. Homelessness, crime, and drug addiction all have one thing in common: social maladjustment, the roots of which are often found in the problems of the family. A socially maladjusted child or youth is a victim whose rights to full development and self-realization in society have been severely violated. When a child becomes a law breaker, she is, in essence, signaling the society that her own rights have been violated.

The pervasiveness of poverty in Russia requires many parents to work two or three jobs simultaneously, allowing them little time to spend with their children and to monitor their behavior properly. Separated, single parents, because of stress, anxiety, or depression, tend to be rude and aggressive and often become a direct source of violence against their own children. A 2002 analysis of household budgets showed that families with children comprised almost 59 percent of all families with per capita household incomes lower than the subsistence minimum. Extremely poor families with resources lower than the subsistence minimum by a factor of two made up 70 percent.[10]

The number of parents and guardians who fail to fulfill or unreliably fulfill their child-rearing responsibilities continues to grow, according to reports of police (MVD) agencies. In 1996 the internal affairs agencies of the Russian Federation investigated 182,700 parents who failed to fulfill their responsibilities; the number had increased to 280,700 in 2002.[11] Each year the number of abandoned children grows—in 2000, there were 123,000—and the number of court actions/prosecutions involving the revocation of parental rights is also increasing, from 19,800 in 1998 to 43,100 in 2002.[12]

Homelessness

Child homelessness is defined in Russia in two ways. First, as the homeless or neglected youth (*beznadzornyi*) who is a minor and whose parents or legal guardians fail to fulfill or reliably fulfill their child-rearing responsibilities and therefore there is no control over the child's behavior. *Bezprizornyi*—a more commonly used term in Russia—is a *beznadzornyi* who lacks a place of residence. This usually refers to orphans and in some instances to children who have no place to sleep.[13] For our purposes we will employ the term "homelessness" to refer to both Russian terms whether or not the child has a home or a bed.

RESEARCH TRENDS AND CRIMINAL CASES

In the last decade, sociologists and psychologists have begun to focus more attention on the problem of abuse and, in particular, abuse of the least protected member of society—the child. Theoretical elaborations of the concept of family abuse and its manifestations have reached a rather sophisticated level. Now the phenomenon is researched within the frameworks of several disciplines, including psychology, sociology, medicine, and criminal law. Although intentional or premeditated violence against children may be hard to fathom, it is a serious and growing problem. Sociological research underscores the fact every year millions of minors are subjected to abuse by family members.

Establishing a direct link between family abuse and homelessness is difficult because the abuse is hidden within and confined to the family. We can only scratch the surface of the problem by examining the cases of cruel treatment of children reflected in the MVD reports or cases of heinous crimes such as murder and torture wherein the victims are children and the perpetrators are either their parents or guardians. Such behavior is accepted by children as normal because they are not aware of other forms of treatment by family members. Medical records indicate that children often enter the hospital with signs of severe physical abuse. For example, traces of torture and mutilation are found on their bodies, as well as evidence that they were nearly starved to death.[14]

An example of such abuse was reported by the PDN, OVD[15] or units within the MVD agencies that deal with youth, in April 2003. For the purposes of confidentiality, we will call this boy Demyan.

A thirteen-year-old boy named Demyan missed school several times a week. His mother, a doctor by profession, told her son's teacher that when he takes a long walk and comes home, he then goes to school. After being away for a longer time than normal and missing numerous school days, Demyan finally showed up. He was very tense, appeared sick, and lost consciousness during class. The medical authorities uncovered several bruises and abrasions on the child's body. The boy stated that his mother beat him with a stick because he took 500 rubles from her. He left home. Such conflicts with the mother, combined with beating, happened frequently and drove the child to the streets.

PROFILE OF AN ABUSED, HOMELESS CHILD

Nearly 80 percent of the children requiring social services use alcohol, toxicants, narcotics, and cigarettes. Many of them have already broken the law and the majority of others are potential law breakers.[16] Parents who force their children to beg on a regular basis essentially groom them to become homeless juvenile offenders whether they realize it or not. The child is on the street, as a rule, for a long period of time and his territory changes and expands over time. The majority of children who beg are very young, six to ten years of age. After learning to get money "the easy way," with age the child expands his sphere of activity and territory and adapts to this lifestyle. Having learned how to survive, children are reluctant or refuse to go to a shelter or other institution because they know that their freedom will be curtailed. They are used to doing what they want, when they want, and those habits are hard to change.

METHODOLOGY AND FINDINGS

A multifaceted methodology was used to determine the degree and mechanisms of the influence of family violence on child homelessness. Sociological research tools, such as surveys of those working within the PDN, OVD with children of potential or previous vulnerability or "weakened social immunity" to homelessness, were used. In addition, criminal court cases of abusive behavior against minors and criminal cases of crimes committed by abused minors revealed that they were subjected to cruel treatment for a long period of time. Court-appointed psychiatric experts examined the victims and juvenile offenders and their reports provided valuable insight into the children's psychological profiles. Finally, there was an analysis of special operations where investigators entered homes of persons suspected of neglect of parental child-rearing practices.

Surveys

Thirty respondents of the surveys were PDN, OVD staff workers within the regional Administration of Internal Affairs and local MVD agencies responsible for preventing homelessness. They were asked about the links between family abuse and homelessness and how this is illustrated in their special raids and operations, their study of children who willingly leave home regularly and are homeless. In addition, psychologists and staff workers at special, closed schools for juvenile offenders in Irkutsk were polled about the ties between abuse and homelessness and about the features of their families.

The connection between family violence and child homelessness is illustrated in a survey of respondents who worked at special closed schools for juvenile offenders (*TsVINPy* or *Tsentry vremennoy izolatsy nesovershennykh pravonarushiteli*). The survey shows that almost 90 percent of the youth experienced violence against them by their close relatives and that running away from home in protest against physical abuse was a regular occurrence.

The youth spoke boldly about the relationship with their parents, often calling their mothers "good" and "kind" in situations where the reality was completely different. Children ages eight to nine spoke about physical abuse whereas older children tended to speak about psychological violence, such as the threat of beating and the threat of being thrown out on the street, beaten up, and isolated if some request of the parent or guardian were not fulfilled. Very little was said about sexual abuse, but this cannot be excluded.

Court-Appointed Psychiatric Expertise and Criminal Cases

One of the most reliable and convincing methods of determining the impact of abuse on the child is the study of reports prepared by court-appointed psychiatric experts. The psychiatric reports on juvenile criminals analyzed were those of closed criminal court cases in the city of Irkutsk and Irkutsk oblast between 1997 and 2002. They represent solidly based, comprehensive research because they include the mandatory participation of psychologists and contain rather thorough analyses of the children's pubescent development, family characteristics, and relationships within the family. The research focused on youth offenders in Irkutsk City and Irkutsk oblast (province) who had adapted very poorly socially and, most important, had used psychotropic substances: narcotics and toxicants such as sniffing glue, inhaling poisonous gas fumes, and drinking alcohol. Thirty percent developed dependence on narcotics or toxicants. The other control group of 90 percent of the youth suffered from chronic alcoholism.

Special Operations/Raids

One measure of the extent of homelessness is the number of children uncovered by the MVD units during their special operations to establish the identity and whereabouts of missing children as well as those in social shelters or orphanages in Irkutsk Oblast. Their regularly conducted operations to prevent homelessness—such as *"Brodyaga"* and *"Besprizornik"*—illustrate that homeless children can be divided into three basic categories: children who are always on the street (usually more than one to two months); children who are periodically on the street (usually when parents are intoxicated, when conflicts with parents or legal guardians arise, or after a beating); and minors who regularly go home to sleep but for whom all other needs are met on the street.

An analysis of these law enforcement reports reveals that 30 percent of the children leave home because of regular abuse by parents, 30 percent suffer from what specialists call "Wandering Syndrome," and the remaining 40 percent suffer from a variety of other family dysfunctions and other problems. However, the results of these operations reveal only the tip of the iceberg. In order to render an accurate accounting of the scale and scope of homeless children and dysfunctional families, ongoing, frequent investigations are needed.

The data of the MVD youth affairs units of Irkutsk oblast indicate that the number of criminal cases opened on the basis of article 156— "Failure to Rear Children Responsibly"—grew steadily between 1997 and 2000 and then began to taper off.[17] In 1997 forty-nine cases were opened, in 1998 there were eighty-eight cases, and in 1999 there were seventy-seven. By 2000, the number of such cases declined by 10 to 12 percent, which corresponds with the general tendency of fewer crimes being reported and registered than have actually occurred.

How did this happen? Why do the statistics reveal only a few instances of parents being held accountable for these crimes when family abuse is so widespread? There are several explanations.

It is important to note that a serious preventive mechanism for law enforcement work/investigation in this area is hindered by a shortage of special services, an absence of a single coordinated system of exposing these facts, and proof and means of bringing the guilty parties to account for their crimes of neglecting parental responsibilities in child rearing, particularly if such actions are combined with cruel treatment of their children. Law enforcement agencies note the difficulties of collecting evidence that could help them solve crimes and bring the members of a family to court for failing to fulfill or fulfill properly their child rearing responsibilities.

RESEARCH FINDINGS

In nearly 90 percent of the cases examined in Irkutsk city and oblast, there was evidence of a link between family abuse and the child's decision to leave home. An elaboration of this general finding is illustrated in the following:

- Abuse against fourteen- and fifteen-year-old minors usually went on for several months, especially against minors between the ages of sixteen and seventeen, who sometimes experienced such abuse for three to five years. Nearly 90 percent of the minors were physically abused, 88 percent were psychologically abused (including 72 percent who were subject to both forms of abuse), and 4 percent were sexually abused.

- Criminal abuse against children fell out in the following way: complete families, 9 percent; families in which the mother or father is replaced by a father-in-law or mother-in-law, 68 percent; "incomplete" families, 23 percent (20 percent in cases with no mother and 3 percent in cases with no father).

- Sexual crimes against children usually are committed by parents or guardians. Statistics reveal that such crimes are much more frequent in families where there are stepparents or in single-parent families than they are in "whole" families. For example, only 9 percent of the crimes were committed in "whole" families, whereas 68 percent of the crimes were committed in families in which the mother or the father had been replaced with a stepfather or stepmother.

- According to law enforcement practitioners, many crimes are uncovered by accident—usually when the victim becomes pregnant or after a victim has been harmed or murdered. Because they are ashamed, it is very rare for minors to reveal that they have been sexually abused by a father, stepfather, or uncle. In Germany, for example, the correlation of documented cases of family sexual abuse against minors and the number exposed varies as dramatically as 17:1 or 20:1.[18] Physical abuse of minors by family members in the form of beatings occurs in 64 percent of the cases and the denial of food, water, and heat occurs in 8 percent of the cases.

- Tying down, confinement to a dark place, restriction of movement, and other methods are characteristic, according to the author's data, in 4 percent of the cases.[19]

- There are also cases whereby children witness family violence—particularly the beating of wives by their husbands. Children, in some cases, may grow to accept this behavior as normal and this may lead to family violence being perpetuated over time.

According to our research, 50 percent of the abuse cases were related to alcoholism. It is important to underscore that it is not the misuse of alcohol alone on the part of the parents that is the main reason why a child leaves home, but rather the consequences of the drinking: neglect of their parental responsibilities, poor behavior, inability to hold down jobs, and material shortages (poverty). Most of the youth respondents said that they left home due to fear of beating, not wanting to live with stepparents, quarrels with parents or quarrels between their parents, parents' threats to make them leave home, hunger, and harassment.

In families of single mothers, alcoholism is less pervasive and was encountered in 40 percent of the cases. In full families alcoholism was encountered in more than 70 percent of the cases and became the basic reason for the social maladjustment of the youth.

An example is found in a criminal case described below. For the purposes of confidentiality, we will call the boy Ivan.

A young boy of fifteen years named Ivan, suffering from addiction to toxins and held accountable for the cruel murder of his peer, came from a single-parent family consisting of his mother and his grandmother. The whereabouts of the biological father were unknown. Both the mother and grandmother drank hard liquor frequently and lived on the grandmother's pension. Ivan was essentially homeless, because there was no control over his behavior. A violated mechanism of social adaptation did not delay him from becoming an addict of toxins by the time he was fourteen.

According to the reports of the PDN he became a drug distributor. The youth's mother warned the Commission of Minors' Affairs [KDN]. Yet the youth himself revealed in an interview that when he came home periodically, his mother was usually drunk. He reacted violently to her drunkenness and on one occasion took a stick and beat his sleeping mother and grandmother. His systematic absences from home and physical violence toward relatives were a form of protest against their alcoholism.

In many cases the presence of a romantic partner not related to the youth worsens the situation. Frequently, the partners in these families were alcoholics and/or abused the children. In many instances, parental rights are revoked as a juridical fact; however, in practice, the child is not placed in a new home and stays at home periodically when the mother or father are sober—which is rare.

Approximately 15 percent of cases of maltreatment, which is especially acute in the families of single mothers, were tied to the psychological problems of the parents. In 13 percent, treatment was linked to the parent's irritation and desire to get rid of the child.

CONCLUSIONS

This research confirms the existence of indirect links between family misfortune and various forms of asocial behavior in children. Analyses reveal that 70 percent of the families have some form of misfortune. In 40 percent of the cases, child offenders are homeless. Criminal records relating to actual cases of family abuse reveal that in 90 percent of the cases, there are linkages between abuse and the child's decision to leave home. Approximately 13 percent of the children living in shelters had suffered from incest and 10 percent behaved in a manner that suggested that they had been sexually abused in the past.[20]

Family misfortune is more likely to occur in single-parent families—in most cases when the mother is supporting children alone. Family misfortune is also manifested in cases of inverted family functions, such as the grandmother raising the children, alcoholism of both parents (drug addiction was more rare), and in situations involving families with hidden psychological problems and poor intrafamily relations.

Many children, especially those of younger age, treat violent or abusive behavior by their parents as the norm. This is not unusual if we consider the psychological profile of a youth who is only beginning to develop the capacity for concrete thoughts and automatically adapts to the patterns of behavior he or she observes in the family. Specialists have shown that in some instances, youth answer questions about family relationships to the effect that everything is good, but add phrases such as, "Mama sometimes beats me with a stick, if I don't listen."

President Vladimir Putin's commitment to child protection is difficult to measure. In 2002, he publicly allocated 3,189,000 rubles from Presidential Reserve Funds to the Ministry of Labor and Social Protection for social protection of children.[21] How the ministry is implementing social protection of children is not clear. A major impediment to caring for children is the lack of clearly defined roles and authority. Several articles on dealing with homelessness, for example, have shown that the new law on combating homelessness and juvenile crime empowers the MVD, Ministry of Education, Ministry of Justice,

Procuracy, Ministry of Labor and Social Development, Ministry of Health, and Commission on Juvenile Affairs (KDN) to address the problem.

Although family abuse and child homelessness are major issues that may have a devastating impact on the future of Russian society and the health of its human capital, funding for these social needs compete with other federal priorities in the social sphere, such as poverty and services for the physically challenged as well as key strategic goals of combating terrorism and maintaining defense readiness.

It is too simple to dismiss family abuse as confined to the family and therefore not society's or the world's problem. The plight of abused children is getting more publicity in many countries and the presence of unprotected and highly vulnerable street children as fodder for exploitation by criminal groups is visible and real. We hope that our governments will do what they can to continue to publicize these atrocities and find ways of criminalizing negligent and abusive behavior of parents and permitting children to experience childhood without violence or fear.

Chapter 7

Options for the Abandoned Child

I did not get much help once I left the orphanage. Oh, they promised us a job in a shoe factory if we'd go through the training, and an apartment of our own. The orphanage was tough for me. Anything that was ever mine was stolen, so I stole too. That's how I got things. I wanted to get the training and the job, and I did. But they did not tell me that the money I would make would not be enough to live on and that the apartment was going to be so far away. I have to take the bus and the tram to get there and it often takes two hours to arrive at work. My apartment is small and I am not a good cook. They did not teach cooking at the orphanage. I eat chips, crackers, and bread a lot. On the streets, I can make more money.

—Katya, 1999

In the introduction to this book, I revealed how my fieldwork in Moscow naturally led to questioning the future of abandoned children as happy, healthy, and productive citizens. In this chapter I will attempt to outline the paths open to orphans and street children once they leave school. I will also attempt to give an account of the children's experiences once they commit to a path. Of course, there are as many possible lives as there are children, and only the most common experiences can be described in a chapter.

Once abandoned children come of age, it is hard to imagine how they might fit into mainstream society, and the fact is, they do not. Mentally disabled children leaving their institutions at age eighteen (and often sooner) make up the following statistics:

- 18.3 percent become vagrants
- 10 percent become involved in crime
- 10 percent commit suicide[1]

THE MILITARY "OPTION"

The fact is, whether mentally disabled or not, whether in institutions or living on the streets, there are few options for abandoned children as they enter adulthood. At the age of eighteen, young men are required to serve in the military. For those who have family support and money, paying your way out of military duty or signing up for university study may get you out of it. The military is only able to sign up 11 percent of the draftees.[2] For the abandoned, there is no option, as they can neither pay their way out nor commonly enroll at a university to use student status as an excuse. Many who refuse to fulfill their military duty might feign suicide and end up in an insane asylum—a preferred place to the troops. Life in the Russian military for some is their worst nightmare come true, while for others it is a place that offers shelter and food. Given the fact that some can pay their way out, the ones who do end up joining are often the least educated, poorest, and most desperate. In 2002, Defense Minister Sergei Ivanov noted that those who are drafted are often in such poor condition that they need months of supplementary nutrition to get into shape.[3] A contributing detriment is that the nutrition is notoriously bad in the army, consisting for the most part of watered-down soup and bread.

There are at least three obvious problems inherent in Russian military culture that contribute to the horrendous conditions. Most frightening to young conscripts is the practice of *dedovschina*, or hazing. It is a tradition that is known to have started in the 1960s but possibly earlier. Hazing involves second-year conscripts beating and humiliating the first-year conscripts. After the first year, the now-second-year conscripts achieve the status of the ones beating and humiliating and so the process continues and is reinforced. Maiming and even murder have been associated with this tradition, which has led to mass desertion.

Far worse than soldiers beating soldiers is that officers sometimes beat soldiers. Then the soldiers have nowhere to go to complain. Now mothers are uniting to fight for their children's rights in the military, but it's not enough.[4]

The Committee of Soldiers' Mothers of Russia, led by Maria Kirbasova, formed in 1989 to protect the rights of sons in the Russian military. So far these mothers have worked hard to inform families of servicemen about specific conscripts' health, location, and conditions. They have staged public events and campaigned for the reorganization of the military. Among their services are a phone hotline for information about the Chechen conflict and barracks for soldier-fugitives. The barracks offer physical rehabilitation, legal counseling, and employment services.

However, change in the military is slow. In the fall of 2002, fifty-four young men deserted the army. According to news broadcasts, it was the largest desertion ever to be made public in Russia. Many have remained secret. Accompanying the 2,270 deserters within the first half year of their duty, there are the recorded eighty-nine soldiers who committed suicide in the first six months of 2002 and 127 noncombat-related deaths.[5] Frequently the deserters are caught and brought back to their units where they face possible death by more beatings. Only money can sometimes save the conscripts from these punishments, but this is certainly not an option for the homeless children joining the troops, as they have no outsiders to support them financially.

A second problem with the Russian military is a perceived attempt to win wars by numbers. As one Russian émigré noted:

No matter what the official military doctrine says, Russian soldiers have been and still are considered cannon fodder. Russians have always won wars (often thoughtlessly) throwing hoards of soldiers' lives into the war grinder until the enemy simply chokes. This is especially true for the twentieth century. While this strategy is inhumane, it has proven to be very effective. As much as I hate to say it, I do believe if it wasn't for this "unbeatable" strategy, World War II would have ended differently.[6]

The masses of homeless and abandoned children joining the troops are primarily abused, not trained. They find themselves in a no-win situation.

Finally, overall Russian military corruption has victimized those at the bottom ranks. Citizens fear that the corruption is even worse than what is generally found in Russian society. Of the forms of corruption mentioned in interviews, looting, extortion, illegal searches and confiscations, lynching, and spontaneous executions are known to have occurred in Chechnya. This corruption is rumored to have aided the very people Russians are fighting. One confidant explains:

Since everything can be bought and sold, soldiers are often supplied with old weapons, since those in charge are cautious (and rightly so!) of sending modern arms to Chechnya. A recent event with a suicide bombing of a government building in Grozny that killed almost 90 people proves it once again . . . those trucks were supposed to be thoroughly searched at three military checkpoints![7]

For food, cigarettes and drink, ammunition, and firearms may be sold to the enemy, leading to further corruption.

Before, after, and instead of military duty, most abandoned children are drawn to the criminal world. Many dream of becoming highly respected criminals. They dream of becoming hired killers, preferably overseas (in the United States), and earning both fame and fortune for their murders. It is as if human life is dispensable. While their own survival is the goal, deaths of others are shrugged off as part of life. Many abandoned children appear cold to the violence surrounding them and eagerly find a place for themselves in the criminal hierarchy.

THE CRIME OPTION

Itar-Tass reported that more than 100,000 crimes were committed by teenagers in Russia in 1999, which made up approximately 13 percent of all crimes. Of these crimes, 3,119 were in Moscow and of this, 1,894 were categorized as "grave."[8] Most of these teenage crimes have been attributed by the Office of the Prosecutor-General in Russia to the abandonment of the children by their parents.

Since the fall of the Soviet regime, Russia has become notorious for its mafia. The mafia is an organized crime ring that operates at almost all levels of society, reaping benefits of both large and small businesses and manipulating government activity. As one business owner explains:

I am not involved in the mafia any more than everyone else is these days. They come to you and offer security for your business for a fee. If you refuse to pay, then they will bomb your business, and you will pay them the next time to avoid future attacks. They come to you no matter how small you are; even a kiosk gets offered "protection."[9]

Every business, from the international to the small kiosk, is threatened by the mafia. The mafia deals with all levels of society and consists of various levels, from the head to the "feeder." This is no different than what occurred prior to Mikhail Gorbachev. Under the Soviet regime, the higher-ranking government officials were known to make their fortunes by establishing a following of supporters and maintaining a culture of blackmail, extortion, and bribery. Many of these same government officials are also today's leading criminals.

Today, these high-ranking members of the mafia are the heroes and employers of the feeders: the abandoned and youth. Establishing a name among your peers on the streets and a leader in criminal activity, means opening doors to future higher callings in the criminal world. In order to gain this position and title, a youngster must stop at nothing to win the respect of his or her peers. Missions from small muggings to beatings are not given a second thought and are accomplished and noted, depending on their noteworthiness. Some beatings are done simply for fun, reminiscent of scenes in Anthony Burgess' novel *A Clockwork Orange* in which the speaker initially enjoys spending his evenings attacking innocent people in various bloody ways. Gosha, an abandoned boy, describes:

When we go out, we are out until evening. We find some drunken woman or crap on an old lady. An old lady is walking along: "Hello granny, how are you doing?" She says, "Thanks sonny, I'm fine." Then I go up to her and grab her hat and start tossing it around. She starts running after it. It's interesting. Or a drunk is lying around. I go up and hit him in the face. He gets on his feet and I get him in the back. He goes flying into a tree. It's cool. We can do that all day long.[10]

Today's street child may find joy in the actual attack, so much that it becomes a game and demonstration of one's toughness as well as, in their minds, a display of youth control over the adult world.

THE PROSTITUTION OPTION

Street children do not think of themselves as children. They grew up when they became independent of their parents. The only problem they encounter is how to survive, or better yet, how to live a decent life, despite the adult world's prejudices: As minors they are not allowed to earn a proper living and are forced to find innovative means to earn money. Unfortunately, the possibilities are limited and besides crime, prostitution is often seen as the best solution.

As a result of the created need for prostitution due to adult stigmatization of abandoned children and lack of social support, prostitution has become an industry in Russia. In Moscow alone, there are an estimated 15,000 prostitutes and about 120 brothels. In 2000, a friend took me on an excursion of Moscow's underworld. He pointed to the approximately ten hotels and massage salons that engage in the elite sex business, supposedly controlled by Chechen and Daghestani groups. Most of prostitution takes place on the street or at railroad stations. It is here that street children take part. It is also considered the cheapest and most risky in terms of disease.

Among those scholars studying abandonment of children, the concern for those children who are victims of prostitution is essential for a deeper understanding of the reality homeless children face. Prostitution tends to be treated similarly throughout the world and only rarely do scholars consider the cultural context. While some consistency exists cross culturally, when one does include culture in the analysis of prostitution, it becomes clear that both reasons and solutions for the problem should not, and indeed cannot, be generalized.

Certainly all child prostitutes face similar issues. They are victims and they are all at risk for STDs and other diseases and viral infections. Most will not go on to live "normal" healthy lives, and indeed, many will die before they are adults themselves. Many will have children who will become feeders for the prostitution industry.

Turning specifically to Russia, there remains a mythology surrounding prostitution that both children and adults buy into, thereby hiding the deeper issues and catalysts of the crisis. It is often believed that prostitution is a direct outcome of a developing country. In Russia, prostitution can be traced back historically to the eighteenth and nineteenth centuries. Interestingly, both the industry of prostitution and society's taboo against it were already present at that time. On the one hand, prostitutes became viewed as a necessity to males' sexual needs, and on the other hand, they were seen as a threat to public health and social stability.[11] In order to combat the threat, prostitutes were segregated in various ways from society by such means as, for example in the nineteenth century, relegation to brothels only, with strict rules for conduct and medical treatment.[12] It appears then, that tradition has influenced current perceptions of the industry of prostitution in Russia, rather than Western propaganda, mass media, and the like.

It is also largely believed in Russia that prostitutes are women (men are rarely acknowledged to be part of the industry, a cultural taboo in and of itself) who are destined to prostitute themselves due to their genetic makeup or because they have been raised to work in such a capacity. Accordingly, people assume that many women work as prostitutes because they want to do so. Once again, this belief can be traced back historically in Russia: Prostitutes were believed to have been "tricked into acting sexually—against their nature—or, at the other extreme, as depraved by definition."[13] That is, there exists an impression that women choose prostitution if they are, for one reason or another, programmed to do so.

Unfortunately, many women do not choose to prostitute themselves and even if they do, most do not foresee a life as victims of violence.

Yet, since 1989 the trafficking in women and children from Russia abroad has exploded. Here are some facts:

- In 1989, 378 women from the former Soviet Union entered Japan on entertainment visas. In 1995, 4,763 Russian women entered Japan on entertainer's visas.[14]
- In 2000, it was estimated that 1 to 2 million women and children were forced into prostitution annually, with 45,000 to 50,000 Russian women and children ending up in the United States.[15]
- In 1997, criminal groups made an estimated $7 billion annually by trafficking in women from Russian and other former Soviet republics.[16]
- A woman is worth about $15,000 in the slave industry.

Most women and girls enter the slave industry with other goals in mind: They are offered jobs abroad as maids or bar waitresses. Some even envision a life as a dancer in a bar but do not consider the possibility of prostitution. Others are fully aware that they may end up under the authority of a pimp yet are unaware of the abuse that comes with the job.

Once a woman has responded to an ad and finds herself in a foreign country, working in a bar or even simply upon arrival, she is confronted by her "owner" who will declare himself as such, often destroying her passport and papers in front of his new victim. A women in such a situation understands that she risks her life if she tries to flee. If she refuses to prostitute herself she is beaten and raped:

The efficient, economically brutal routine . . . rarely varies. Women are held in apartments, bars and makeshift brothels; there they service, by their own count, as many as fifteen clients a day. Often they sleep in shifts, four to a bed. The best that most hope for is to be deported after the police finally catch up with their captors. . . . Few ever testify. Those who do risk death.[17]

Prior to accepting a position abroad, many young women dream of even prostitution as a glamorous job in which they will earn a lot of money and possibly find a rich man to marry. Very few foresee the pain that goes with having fifteen clients a day, the beatings dependent on the pimp's whim, the lack of individual freedom, and the prison that awaits them if they are found. Once in prison, they confront deportation to their country of origin where a critical issue remains: How to face the reality of their past.

PRISON LIFE

With a rise in prostitution and pornography among youth comes the rise in juvenile crime, composing a significant proportion of the national total of crimes. While juvenile crime is becoming more complex and widespread, there exists to date an absence of a justice system to handle the cases. With overcrowding of youth facilities and rehabilitation programs, many boys and girls are sent straight to prison for detention until a better option, such as transferal to a youth colony, is found. While thousands of children serve prison sentences in special colonies for juveniles, many more wait in pretrial detention centers with adult inmates. Regardless of the crime, in either facility children are vulnerable to abuse by both guards and other inmates.

The experiences of children in detention centers can be seen not only as in direct opposition to the UN Convention on the Rights of the Child, which ruled that children are entitled to special protection, but also as a general abuse of human rights in general. As children, they are weaker and consequently more vulnerable to abuse suffered by inmates. A former convict explained to me in an interview:

It's like this: You can't be weak in prison. You get thrown into this huge room where there are three times as many people as beds. There were two floors where I was, and we slept in shifts. If you were considered weak, your sleep would be deprived and the weakest was forced to sleep next to the toilet and was also used as the hall's "girl," if you know what I mean. . . . We played cards and drank this tea brew . . . stuff so strong, it would make you high. . . . Being a good card player got me through my time there. But if you upset any of the big guys, your life would be at risk. The guards did not care if you were brutalized. One guy was killed. They threw him from the second floor and said he fell. No one cared.[18]

In Russia, children are held in various types of detention facilities for months at a time. The experience negatively affects the children both physically and emotionally. Emotionally, they are scarred and will have a harder time integrating into society. Physically, they may have been exposed to and contracted various diseases:

According to official Russian sources, over half of Russia's 900,000 men, women and children in prison are ill, with more than one in ten suffering Tuberculosis and around one in 20 suffering from HIV/AIDS.[19]

Prison has the potential of ruining Russia's youth's chances for success in society, yet little is done to change the system.

RUSSIA AND PSYCHOLOGY

This lack of attention given to juvenile crime from an emotional and psychological perspective is in part the result of yet another Russian social taboo: The belief that psychological counseling is inefficient and stigmatizing. Psychology remains a large unknown to Russian citizens. Prior to the Soviet regime, Russian psychology began to bloom with a number of psychologists entering Western scholarly discussion in the field. Such names included Gerory I. Chelpanov (1862–1936), Ivan M. Sechenov (1829–1905), Ivan Pavlov (1849–1936), and Vladimir Bekhterev (1857–1927). However, these psychologists were not in the business of applying psychology in therapy, a later development in the history of psychology, but rather, they debated philosophical issues and conducted psychological experiments. As a result, psychology remained a scholarly rather than a popular field of enterprise.[20]

Under the Soviet regime, psychologists were forced into a new agenda, that of proving psychology's importance to political goals of building communism. The promotion of psychology as a practical and helpful science was faced under Stalin with a most difficult hurdle: to persist under the Stalinist perspective of "the ideal Soviet citizen" as a type, denying psychology's basic premise of personality and individual difference.[21] In fact, those scholars involved in the study of psychology were often repressed and feared for their lives. Stalin haunted both the field of psychology and the psychologists themselves, as he felt threatened by both the theories and diagnoses. According to one "hearsay report," the famous psychologist Bekhterev expressed his own views on the psychological state of Stalin in 1927. His conclusion: Stalin was paranoid. It has been further surmised that as a result of this diagnosis combined with the fact that Stalin was jealous of Bekhterev's reputation, Stalin had Bekhterev immediately poisoned.[22] Repression and terror, characteristic of Stalin's power, stifled the practice of psychology, which to this day is approached with trepidation in Russia.

During the 1920s, debates on the theory and applicability of psychology raged. These debates have been elaborated upon and documented since then,[23] but they came to a screeching halt in 1930, when Stalin denounced psychoanalysis and forbade even mention of Freudian theory, unless it was to criticize pre-Soviet or non-Soviet societies. From an intellectual perspective, Stalinism in and of itself opposed the basis for psychoanalysis. Instead, the individual was shunned and the mainstream Soviet group identity heralded. Citizens were no longer taught to think for themselves, but rather to learn through rote memorization. It was a time when the human individual was forced into a mold, when personal needs were ignored and changed to meet the needs of the regime. Whereas psychoanalysis supports individuality and truth in experience, Stalinism stood for communality and propaganda:

Psychoanalysis was incompatible . . . with a policy of adapting human needs to inhuman conditions. It was incompatible with propaganda about the joys of motherhood and family, because it revealed the "shameful" truth behind that propaganda—the psychosexual tensions within family relationships and the psychic damage inflicted on children by a traditional family upbringing. It was incompatible with sexual Puritanism and with criminalizing sexual behavior like homosexuality. It was incompatible with ignorance about the sexual needs of children and with mistreating them because of that ignorance.[24]

Under Stalinism, the mention of psychoanalysis ceased to exist in Russia.

Today, instead of consulting a therapist, Russians tend to turn to more traditional healers including hypnotists, shamans, and astrologists, or simply to their family and friends. After the Soviet regime, any word drawn from the root "psycho" was under suspicion. After all, if you had any affiliation with "psycho," you could be institutionalized, a fate no one desired. While today more people are growing open to therapy, a general haze remains around the word. Psychology is still not clearly understood by the average citizen.

Instead, the population follows psychological fads. Borrowing from the West, psychotherapists, with little training and much less academic preparation, conduct sessions aimed to relieve their needy patients quickly and efficiently. The thought of long-term, pricey therapy is not easily embraced by a population that lacks funding for and understanding of a complex field of study. An obvious outcome of this lack of awareness in Russia is the lack of psychological support given to the neediest and poorest in the nation. Abandoned children simply do not have access to this kind of help, and if they do, the quality of care is questionable.

With little emotional or educational support, very few abandoned children have access to the intelligentsia. Rarely does a child make it through school and begin university study. More commonly, at the age of fifteen, students enter a vocational school to learn a practical trade. While some learn carpentry or plumbing, others learn skills that are specific to the needs of a particular factory. Upon completion of such training for a factory, students are guaranteed both housing and a job. Unfortunately, housing is not necessarily near the place of work and pay is minimal.

Stories about students' experiences in factories abound. Usually these young adults receive little guidance once they leave their schools and have difficulty caring for themselves, arriving at work, and, in general, making ends meet. In one case, a young woman felt pressure to make more money and rise beyond the limits of her factory job. Feeling that there was no hope in sight, even after her training, she decided to prostitute herself.[25] With only job-specific training, most abandoned youths do not have any hope for upward mobility and certainly cannot rely on their factories to keep them financially stable. Once again, the temptation to make crime and prostitution a source of income is alluring and causes many of those, who once sought employment through education, to give up.

THE ADOPTION OPTION

Russian orphans dream of being adopted by a Western family. As they get older, this dream begins to fade as they come to realize that mostly babies and small children are adopted. Since the fall of the Soviet regime, Russian orphans have found homes throughout the world, including the United States. From 1993 to 1995, the number of orphans adopted from Russia in the United States increased by over 200 percent, from 746 orphans in 1993 to 2,454 in 1996.[26] Adoptions from Russians have continued to rise steadily, from 3,816 in 1997 to 4,491 in 1998, with a slight drop to 4,348 in 1999.[27] Along with the increase, however, come the sad stories of child abuse and neglect the children experienced in their former homeland as well as in their newly found American families. We do know that while life back in Russia continues to be difficult for homeless and institutionalized children, prospects for such children in the United States are more positive than negative. While the media in the United States and Russia continue to sensationalize the hardships many children face in their new American homes, this researcher is finding a perspective on the lives of Russian orphans that differs from that view.

Children adopted by U.S. citizens have the benefit of much cultural change in the last fifty years in the United States. Originally, the North American adoptive family was engineered by social workers who were trying to replicate the American ideal by matching children with their families. Prior to World War II, social workers claimed their role in adoption by not allowing adoptive parents to take home their children until they had been observed for several months and approved as adoptable, with no "deficiencies of intellect, character, or health."[28] Social workers thus proved their role in adoption as indispensable.

In the 1950s caseworkers were concerned about the adoptive mother's mothering potential and looked to her hairstyle and dress being appropriately feminine and insisted that the mother show compassion toward children, domestic skills, and willingness to stay at home. Furthermore, evidence of her inability to bear children herself needed to be proven and an investigation of her cause of infertility needed to be conducted, lest her infertility suggest subconscious reservations about motherhood.[29]

As in Russia, American families often kept their adoption secret. Matching was less important in the late 1950s and 1960s, with the civil rights movement and an increase in families seeking to adopt. However, adoption in American society still meant that one was marked forever,[30] making the naturalness of the adoptive family more complex and the transition to the family unit less fluid.

Today, it is believed that a successful transition for an adopted child must entail first and foremost the support of all involved, especially on the part of both parents. If even one parent has mixed feelings toward the adoptive child, the family as a unit will most likely not feel whole and, moreover, outsiders will view them as not representative of the traditional concept of family.

Research has shown that another crucial component in making the adoptive family a true kinship unit is acceptance by the larger community and, ultimately, by society. Such acceptance rests on a community's ability to redefine traditional terms. In anthropological terms, a family is "a domiciliary and/or kin grouping, variously constituted of married and related persons and their offspring, residing together for economic and reproductive purposes."[31] More specifically, a nuclear family is "a basic social grouping comprising married male and female parents and their offspring."[32] Obviously, these definitions problematize the way society views the adoptive family, for inherent in both of these definitions is the idea that the children must be offsprings, that is, that parents and children share the same blood.

Turning the adoptive family into a true kinship unit further requires that the relatives, community, and society at large rework their understanding of certain components of a traditional family, for example, sharing the same blood will not be present. Virtually every family in this study that had a positive adoption experience and whose family appears to thrive also had strong support from the outside community and extended family.

As societies evolve, so do the definitions of components of a society. Now in the twenty-first century, citizens of the United States are witnesses to the evolution of how we define family structure. As Americans become more open to ethnic, racial, and cultural diversity within families, more children who previously might have fallen into the hands of institutions and/or the foster care system now have the possibility of being adopted.

However, stereotypes of the ideal family and ideal members persist. Much as in Russia, families of adopted children in the United States experience stigmatization. According to parents of adopted children in North America, Americans still do not completely accept the notion that an adoptive child is as "good" as a birth child. In numerous accounts, adoptive parents told of how upon introducing their children as their adopted children, they were asked whether they had any of their own. To some adoptive parents, the assumption that their adoptive child is not their "own" is offensive. Others read into the comment that a birth child would in some way be better than an adopted child, as if the adopted child at birth is impure, or flawed. Adoption is still viewed as a mere humanitarian gesture by some. Although throughout my interviews I came across people who agreed that they could never love their adopted child as they do their birth child, they did not quantify as much as qualify their love. It was not a question of loving a child more or less, but of loving the child differently.

The fact remains that traditional American society in the United States is still developing its complete acceptance of adoptive parents. This is not merely reflected in individual discussion but is communicated by the lack of social norms and laws to accommodate the expecting adoptive couple. Rarely are adoptive parents granted leave to pick up their child, as a mother is to give birth to her child, or after, to give the child some stability before releasing it into the hands of yet another caretaker. In more than one case, an adoptive parent was let go when she pushed to have some time off. Support for adoptive parents is evolving, only slowly.

To speed up the process of social support, adoptive parents have initiated their own traditions. Baby showers are now common prior to the departure of a couple to pick up their child. While birthdays are celebrated, so are adoption dates and the acquisition of U.S. citizenship dates.

Preparing for the arrival of the adopted child is perhaps as laborious as waiting for the birth child. The wait is often longer and the paperwork excruciating. Indeed, the entire process may be compared to pregnancy, demanding the parents exercise both patience and organization skills. From a physical perspective, nesting is common for both birth and adoptive parents. Most adoptive parents will show the picture of the child to their friends and family, just as a birth parent shows the ultrasound to all interested. The baby's room is prepared for the new arrival, as is often the rest of the house with baby proofing and cleaning. Emotionally, both birth and adoptive parents are on roller coasters, at the same time delighted and afraid of what the future holds with the new child. Some parents, again both birth and adoptive, express times of panic as they fear what could go wrong before the arrival or delivery. Frequently adoptive mothers report nausea and the need for fluid and food intake after the confirmation of a referral.

Receiving the child in Russia is no less painful. The final handing over of the child is accompanied by tears of joy and fear. Children often cry hysterically as they are extricated from their orphanage caretakers' arms and out of their old orphanage clothes and placed into new clean outfits and their new parents' arms. Their bodies are often undernourished and many parents note the bones being visible through the translucent skin. The first few nights back in the hotel or with a Russian family in Moscow, as the new families await their papers from the embassy, are fraught with crying and sleepless hours, all of which are reminiscent of the post-birth experience.

After the adoption is complete and the child is at home, parents may choose to create a "Life Book," documenting the child's childhood and adoption. Life Books come premade or homemade. One couple informing this chapter and adopting from China wrote their children's stories in the form of children's books with illustrations.

Coming to the United States

By deciding to adopt, an American family consciously chooses to take a nontraditional path to creating a family. For the adoptive family, there are different challenges, many of which have yet to be studied and addressed in scholarly literature. By choosing to adopt from Russia, American families contend not only with their own social issues, but also with those of Russia as well.

While the process of adoption from Russia is fairly standard, complications with the courts, the federal government, and the children themselves are common. Underlying the Russian government's inconsistent policies was the desire of the government to keep healthy children, a potential and necessary future workforce, in Russia. Even now, children with disabilities are easier to adopt than are healthy, newborn infants. Children suffering from physical or psychological handicaps are given up for adoption with few questions asked.

In one of the stories collected, adoptive parents were told that there were siblings, a boy and a girl, available for adoption. The mother tells:

Apparently they were born to a young mother, perhaps on drugs or drink, who refused to care for them properly. After lengthy absences, the neighbors began to call and complain to authorities that the children were never fed or cared for and they were eventually removed from the home at ages three and one. The boy (Gabe) was sent straight to the hospital with pneumonia and remained there for six months to recuperate, while his younger sister (Kailey) was placed in a baby home. The mother was notified that she had six months to petition the court for their return, but she never tried to contact them and no one has heard from her since. The children were eventually placed up for adoption separately, but there were no families found for them. Kailey was moved over to be with her brother in a children's home and a few months later we were notified that they were available for us, if we were interested.[33]

Upon viewing their potential children with a Russian psychologist, the adoptive parents were advised that Kailey suffered from fetal alcohol syndrome and that the problems the adoptive family faced were possibly insurmountable. After much thought and a few meetings with the children, the family decided to bring Gabe and Kailey home. While the transition was not easy for the children, to date they both continue to thrive with no signs of fetal alcohol syndrome or other handicaps.

In this case, the children were available to Americans because of their age and potential emotional or mental handicaps, as is often the case in Russia, whether or not the handicaps are determined to be true. In fact, orphanages have been known to state on paper that a child is challenged, even when this is not the case, simply so that the child can be adopted internationally.

Two Myths Dispelled

A number of myths (some of which have been mentioned above) persist to feed the stereotypes and subsequent marginalization of adopted children from Russia. Here are a few stories presented in the hopes of dispelling some of the myths.

Myth 1: Adopting an older child from Russia is detrimental to your family life.

Indeed, some older children, especially those who have been abused and neglected, may come with issues that the average family might have difficulty with in trying to integrate the child into family life. However, this is not the case with every older child, as described by the G. family, who adopted ten-year-old D.

On March 27 (2002) my wife and I returned from Russia with our son D. We had just finished a remarkable journey that had taken us from being the host family for our "son-to-be" through an international family service in June of 2001 to where we stand today as D.'s parents.

It all started out innocently enough. We actually found out about the possibility by accident. A friend of ours happened to mention that she and her husband were planning to host two children, a brother and sister from Russia, and that there was still one little boy in need of a host family. After contacting the local office, my wife and I jumped in with ten days to go, whereas the other families had a few months to prepare themselves.

The seventeen little angels arrived at the tiny hamlet in Pennsylvania at 4 A.M. on a warm June morning. Some sleepy, some crying, and all over-tired from what must have seemed a lifetime of travel: Ivanova to Moscow to Dulles, but no connecting flights available to Pittsburgh, so the organization rented vans to carry everyone to western Pennsylvania. A phone tree kept the information flowing to the equally sleepless host families. Then we got the final call: They were a bit less than an hour from the office. It was time to drive over there and join the nervous group of families.

And then it happened: The vans pulled up and the families crowded around the windows of the small second-floor office for that first peek at the youngsters. It was actually difficult to see anything. A local TV station was set up to film the activity as part of a series. . . . Up the narrow stairway they all came and into the office. Seventeen young faces and the three Russian caregiver ladies in an "across the office" standoff with the host families.

The office manager started calling out names and she and her assistant started pairing families with children. A boy scout had prepared backpacks filled with small toys and other goodies for all the children as his eagle scout project. Soon all the adults and children were sitting on the floor going through the packs and getting to know each other. Not withstanding the language difficulty, there were plenty of accented "pleases and thank yous." And so began our journey.

The month passed ever so quickly, but not before my wife and I decided to pursue the tangled web of international adoption. After months of stressful preparation, as I am sure many prospective adoptive families are painfully aware, we boarded a Delta flight . . .

Back at home, D. has adjusted very well. Our next door neighbor's boy is also ten years old and instantly struck up the friendship that began so long ago last summer. The two are together constantly and are joined often by the other boys in the neighborhood. It is quite a gang. Our two golden retrievers are also D.'s best friends, though they do tend to take up significant space on his bed.

School is also going very well for D. Just this last week we had our first face to face parent-teacher meeting, but with a significant twist. In attendance was the Superintendent of the Elementary Schools, the Elementary School Principal, and five of D.'s teachers. Three of these ladies are part of the PA-mandated ESL [English as a Second Language] program. D. is in the fourth grade, doing well, and making friends. The teachers and students love his accent, especially when he rolls his R's. We have been so very fortunate.

Not only does this family feel good about their choice to adopt an older child, moreover, their community of family and friends was supportive, offering encouragement and congratulations.

The Palmers encountered a similar experience with the adoption of Gabe and Kailey (ages five and three). Lisa Palmer elaborates:

These kids needed a great deal of supervision and training at first, but caught on quickly. It took a while for the younger one to be completely dry at night, but she is very successful now and proud of her accomplishment. They were immediate playmates for our daughter and were probably in more "need," as they had been turned down or overlooked by Russian families because they were too old or had trumped-up medical problems. On the other hand, they both came with a package of issues arising from their early abandonment and subsequent institutionalization that younger babies might not have to deal with. In our case, prayer and patience seem to help us overcome, and they all act like normal siblings now.[34]

The Palmers are honest in their recollection of the issues of transition and yet are also proud of their children's accomplishments and aware of their potential as integrated members of American society.

Myth 2: The adopted child will always feel adopted to the mother.

A fear that parents have before adopting is that the child never feel like their own offspring and that the bonding that exists between a birth mother or father and a child may never happen between the adoptive parent and child. However, while one may hear stories supporting this opinion, there is another view. Some parents, especially parents of only adopted children, after a while admit that the adoption part of their children is no longer relevant to their lives, except in conversation about the past. Jane, mother of an adopted girl from Russia, explains:

In the beginning, I think because she felt new to us, we had to tell everyone about her because the experience was so recent. But after a while, it felt as though she had been with us forever and I found myself not wanting to tell people that she is adopted. Now I don't offer the information unless they already know about the adoption. Somehow, by not talking about it, it recedes from our memories too. Looking at our daughter, no one would ever wonder whether or not she is our biological child and most of the time I forget it too. I'll find myself thinking, "she has ears just like my husband" or "her hair is the same color as his." I believe that our daughter came to us through a higher power and that there was no question at all that she was meant to be our daughter. I actually felt that we would adopt before we even began to try to have a child of our own. Maybe it was woman's intuition, I don't know. So, having our daughter feels like the most right thing in the world, like the decision was preplanned for us long before we knew it. On a daily basis, I feel like her mother all the time. Every time she says "mommy," it feels so natural. Now that language is not a barrier, I realize that she understands that everyone has a mommy and daddy and she doesn't seem to remember anyone before us. She loves being around other children and is fascinated by babies and I think this comes from her orphanage days. The only time I fixate on the fact that she is not our biological daughter is when I see her growing and changing and wonder how she'll be as an adult, or how she'll take it when she's old enough to understand that she was adopted and if she'll want to try to find her mother. I know I find myself wondering what her conditions were like and whether her mother will be alive if we go to find her years from now. It would definitely put the question to rest for me as well if we could one day locate her.

The only regret I have is that we could not have had our daughter from a younger age. I often imagine what a beautiful baby she would have been and wish that we could have been there for her sooner. I feel that she had a lot of disappointment in her first two years and wish that we could have prevented some of the abandonment that she experienced.[35]

Jane's feelings—that this baby was her destiny, that she was meant to be her mother—are often felt and expressed by adoptive parents. Predestined to be together, the bond between parent and child is real and on some level natural, even biological, and to the parent, no distinction can be made between birth or adopted.

Even parents with biological children can feel the parental bond with their adopted child, as Lisa Palmer explains:

We felt the responsibility and awe immediately. They were ours and we were responsible for them, for better or worse. . . . The ability to let our guard down and really love them was easy: They had no one else and were all alone in the world. (Besides, they are both really cute!) There was always a favoring toward our natural daughter, if only because she was more capable and could be trusted more, but even that is disappearing as they are venturing out on their own and accomplishing things in their own right. We feel parental pride now, for instance, when all our children passed their swimming lessons. . . . We share in their smiles and sense of accomplishment now, even enjoy watching them interact with others. . . . We are a "normal" family.[36]

In the case of the Palmers, they had been warned by family and friends that adopting Russian orphans, especially older ones, could be detrimental to their "normal" family life and even threatening to their daughter. News reports of adopted children attacking siblings had fueled this concern. However, the news that failed to be reported in the media was the fact that many families enjoy strong bonds with their Russian adopted children.

Challenges of the Russian Adopted Child

While success stories abound, each family will attest to hurdles in the process. Many of the hurdles are the problems the children have, either physical or emotional or both. Some of the emotional and physiological issues the children may have include aggressive or passive behavior, autistic-like behavior, and attachment issues. Sometimes their social skills are lacking and they may show indiscriminate affection. Many of the orphans also have developmental delays and learning disabilities, including hyperactivity, language delays, and cognitive disorders. They may have little sense of cause and effect and possibly no concept of past versus future. Finally, many start their lives in the United States with medical problems such as Hepatitis B and D. Many of these problems are direct results of institutionalization. It is important to remember, however, that not all institutionalized children have these problems.

Babies from institutions have learned that crying does not necessarily lead to a caretaker's attention or even worse, it may result in a negative reaction. As a result, babies learn to shut down when they need help, and when they do have the attention of a caregiver, they hold on for dear life by grabbing and pulling. Their means of communication may become unlike most human communication, that is, more extreme and even aggressive. As one mother describes:

Parents of very young children adopted from institutions usually find that their child is quiet, unemotional, and less reactive than other children of the same age. They are relatively compliant and cooperative. But suddenly, at some point, they get wild. . . . Nobody has taught them how to regulate their responses, how to take turns, how to ask for help or care. They may not know how to take cues from the responses of others to gauge how their behavior is being perceived.[37]

At such a young age, therapy can still be very helpful, as can, in some instances, simply the stability and love of a good home. As they get older in an institution, however, orphans also need to cope with living around many other children, many of whom have problems too. They experience continual lack of privacy and lack of something to call their own. Violence among children, especially older and stronger children threatening and abusing younger and weaker children, is common. Not surprisingly, these children have more difficulty adjusting to their new lives as adopted children.

While physical problems are visible, emotional ones often take time to appear. The greatest fear of adoptive parents, given the focus in the media in the past, is the difficulty of taking in a child with attachment disorder. According to the specialists, this seems to be most common among children who are adopted at a later age. Symptoms of attachment disorder include an inability to give and receive affection, lack of eye contact, indiscriminate affection with strangers, extreme anger, manipulative behavior, stealing, hoarding or gorging food, preoccupation with fire or gore, lack of impulse control and cause and effect thinking, learning and speech disorders, lack of conscience, lying, lack of friends, incessant chatter, being inappropriately demanding or clingy, and hostile or angry behavior. This emotional challenge complicates traditional family life, and yet it must be remembered that only some children adopted from Russia demonstrate various degrees of this disorder.

In Russia, very little comes easily and most people find that "getting around rules and regulations" is the only way to get by. In orphanages, this mantra is even stronger. In order to own something, you must hide it. In order to get something, you must steal it or charm an adult. While you may act like a good child and outwardly do as you are told, getting away with things is the norm. For this reason, adopting older children and especially street children becomes challenging as one tries to teach them to value honesty. Lisa Palmer recalls that "disobedience, disrespect, dishonesty—you name it! There was a much greater need for discipline than we realized, probably due to lack of training in their young lives."[38] What is valued and necessary in order to survive in a Russian orphanage may become a hindrance when trying to integrate into most American families.

Conclusion: Their World Still with Secrets and Sorrow

It is the fall of 2000 in Moscow. My youngest son is just six months old. I am here on assignment with my husband and my job this time is quite different. I am not the student-researcher anymore, but the diplomat's wife, mother of two, and university professor. I no longer need to collect data, but because I am so close, I cannot stop myself from visiting that baby orphanage from my research in 1992. My baby happy for a while with a sitter, I gather my courage and hail a taxi to the place that filled my days and that I remember so well. The taxi drops me off outside the walls and the large metal gates. They are open, and, as I did so often almost a decade ago, I enter.

I notice that not much has changed from the outside: Uncut grass and brush hang over the same old playground toys, the yellow paint of the orphanage remains chipped, perhaps a bit more than then. An elderly lady is sweeping the front steps to the orphanage. Does she remember me? I recognize her as one of the caretakers and ask her if I could meet the director. With few words, she hurries in, only to appear again a minute or so later with the same director I had worked with before, Galina.

Galina is surprised to see me, but not pleased: Am I here to stay again? Were they caught off-guard again? I immediately offer her the gift I had brought, appease her mind, and tell her I am here only to visit. With a sigh of relief, Galina shows me to her office. I notice that the halls are the same, the smell of overboiled meat and potatoes lingers from today's lunch, and indeed, the posh furniture in the director's office is the same. I comment that little has changed, as Galina collects the other doctors to welcome me. Quite the contrary, I am told: A new sauna/steam room (*banya*) has been built, thanks to the donations from the West. It is adjacent to this very office. For the children? Well, yes, sometimes. It is mostly used by the staff. May I see the children? I am told that not much has changed, just the faces.

I cannot resist asking about some of the children I had worked with, whom I had written about in my report to an adoption agency. What about little Tanya, the girl whom no one would adopt in Russia because her ears stood out? Yes, she was now living in the United States. And the boy, Sasha with the cleft palate, who would not stop crying? He, too, had been adopted by a family in Canada. As it turns out, he not only had trouble eating, but seeing too, a fact the Russian orphanage had not known, even with the presence of staff pediatricians. Now he wears glasses and, in a family of three boys, he is known as "the little intellectual," devouring books and taking great pride in his accomplishments. I had always been concerned about Andrei, the boy whose father came as a student from Africa and left again and whose mother could not raise him in her family due to racism and ultimate rejection. Andrei, too, had been adopted and was now doing well in Canada. Unfortunately, Galina, the little girl with cerebral palsy, was presumed dead after suffering from pneumonia. Many others are forgotten by the staff who sees so many children come and go each year. "We remember the ones whose adoptive families write and send photos. We cannot remember them all," Galina reminds me.

Indeed, little to nothing has changed and I cringe at the sight of the infant room. Now a mother myself, I cannot bear the thought of leaving the babies alone in their cribs, crying. I am told, as I was years ago, "We simply do not have the manpower to hold them every time they cry. They have to learn to comfort themselves." I ask if I may hold them; perhaps I could come on a weekly basis, just to hold them? It would be good for them, I know, as I am a mother too: Babies need to be held! Galina asks about the possibility of more diapers. I reply, "I have no contacts to collect diapers. I can ask around. But I am simply asking to hold the babies. I want nothing in return." Galina answers,

"We cannot have complete strangers coming in here holding our babies." "But I am not a complete stranger. I used to live here. I could get you my resume and recommendations from various people at the embassy. In fact, I could organize a few diplomats' wives to come and help me, I am sure!" Indeed, I had heard of such groups being formed and going to hospitals and one other orphanage. "I am sorry. But if you have diapers, or other products or donations, we would be happy to take them. Perhaps we could have tea again. It is so nice to hear about you and your family." Understanding the finality of the unspoken message, I thank the director for her hospitality and leave. Within an hour I am home to embrace and hold my own child.

Enter the year 2004. The year has been filled with articles in newspapers, documentary films on juvenile delinquency and HIV in Russia, and my own continuing interviews with Russian educators and colleagues, and I find again that little has changed. Homeless children are again being hoarded and sent to the outskirts of cities, only to return in droves, to beg, to engage in petty theft, in an attempt to find a kind of life beyond the existence of the orphanage. They engage in petty theft, sell themselves, and prey on others to survive. Many of these teenagers end up in penitentiary institutions, which are still characterized by overcrowding, corruption, and abuse. HIV cases have risen dramatically in the past five years, with the estimated infections at 1 million. The United Nations estimates that, with a population of 145 million people, the cumulative number of AIDS deaths for 2020 will reach 6.9 million and by 2045, 16.4 million. On a positive note, adoptions in Russia have increased, a sign that perhaps the perception of orphans is changing among Russians. However, homelessness and poverty continue to be problems. Child victimization has expanded as, poor or not, children become targets of terror, as was the case in Beslan on September 1, 2004, when armed terrorists from Chechnya, Ingushetia, and other nations took hundreds of school children and adults hostages. After a shootout with the Russian army on the third day, more than 300 civilians were killed, at least 172 of them children. For anyone interested in Russia, be it from a personal or academic perspective, children can no longer be left out of the discussions on social development and culture.

Scholars in the West are coming to see the study of childhood as a vital component to understanding societies and their strengths and weaknesses. Myra Bluebond-Langner, director of Rutgers University's Center for Children and Childhood Studies, predicts that studies of children and childhood are growing in importance so much that they "will be to this century what women's studies was to the last."[1]

We raise and educate children with the assumption that they are like us, only less knowledgeable and, in some people's eyes, more pure. What we do not acknowledge, on neither a personal nor social scientific level, is that children possess a culture of their own, while simultaneously weaving in and out of the culture of adults. While children are continuously being enculturated by the adult world, children also create and develop their own cultures, which are, to some extent, independent of and distinct from those of the adults with whom they live.[2]

As I read over the interviews conducted with young inmates in prisons and on the streets, it is clear that the children themselves are conscious of their own world and needs. They can tell us what they need, so while social scientists continue to grapple for solutions to the growing problem of child abandonment, the answer has always been there. Unfortunately for those struggling on the streets today, remedies and prescriptions of social welfare contexts and social scientists are mere bandages on deeper wounds that may never heal, because, what each and every child expresses is a desperate need to be loved. And yet, neither the orphanages nor other child institutions acknowledge the significance of love. They declare children to be damaged yet make no efforts to "repair" them emotionally, focusing merely on building functional behavior or societal compliance through training. While Makarenko may have been successful in training children to function in society on a superficial level, little is said about their happiness and sense of fitting into a mainstream society.

Unlike Makarenko, there were some well-known Russian thinkers who did acknowledge the voice of children. Such was the case with Kornei Chukovsky, who, in the early 1900s, began writing for children only after having actually studied them. Chukovsky believed that only by studying childhood and its uniqueness can one communicate with children. Unfortunately, his beliefs were not manifested in education or child-care.

More research on child culture has been conducted in the West, by such scholars as Opie and Opie and Virtanen, who have published anthologies of child lore and demonstrate that children do in fact propagate their own culture, distinct from that of adults. Opie and Opie (1969) conducted extensive studies on child lore and child culture. Later, Virtanen (1978) pointed out through similar studies that children perceive the world differently from adults, a claim for which she offers evidence taken from children's language, slang, rhymes, secret clubs, and general peer culture.

However in Russia, few social scientists have listened to the children themselves in studying issues that children face in Russia. Those who have deal mainly with mainstream children who have supportive families. Scholars who have opened their ears and minds to the child's point of view include scholars who acknowledge the existence of a child culture that is different from that of adults. Many of these are psychologists in Russia who follow the research of Dr. Maria Osorina. Like earlier scholars in the West, Osorina today addresses differences between adult and child culture specifically located in speech and activities such as games. Through her research, it is evident that children's behavior, thought, and speech differ from that of adults and may be viewed as semiautonomous subcultures. An anthropologist should no more ignore the existence of a child subculture in a dominant culture than he or she would ignore the relationship of any elite or subaltern group:

Imagine the following scenario: An ethnographer works among a population whose social structure is sharply stratified. One group, whose cultural identity derives from a notion of maturity and attributed competence, wields significant power over a subaltern class, whose identity derives from a notion of immaturity and attributed incompetence. There are culturally specified economic, emotional and social relationships between these two groups, both of whom are named by terms roughly translatable into English terms. . . . In this culture, like many others, the elite talk endlessly about their subaltern clients and seem to derive an important dimension of their sense of self and competency by the relative successes and failures of their clients. . . . Remarkably, the ethnographer never, in all her writings, mentions the subaltern population.[3]

Such a scenario of ignoring an important subculture would be blasphemous, and yet ethnographers through the years have ignored child culture, which, like the subaltern population described above, occupies a great deal of time in society and moreover gives the adult world a sense of self and purpose.

If it can be said that mainstream anthropology has marginalized the study of children, then it can be said doubly for the insights offered into the lives of abandoned children. Very few scholars have addressed the uniqueness and significance to society of abandoned children. Even fewer have acknowledged their distinct cultures and their simultaneous integration and separateness from adult society. From the moment a child is born, she will find her place in the world as a result of her interaction with adults, but more significantly and especially for the abandoned child, also from her peers. For generations children, abandoned or not, have figured out how to create their own secret world. We, too, were once members of this secret world, but over time we have forgotten its worthiness and relevance to understanding our own children and who we are today as a society.[4]

Abandoned children take their secret world to a higher level. Their interaction with the adult world is mainly negative and minimal at best, in large part due to a lack of mutual understanding on both sides. On the one hand, scholars have demonstrated in their writings an existence of social organization among street children, one that entails strong relationships among peers and is supported by networks to ensure the sharing of food and goods. On the other hand, society continues to view and portray street children as a social threat:

[P]opular conceptions of street children frequently portray them as unsocialized or antisocial dangers to the established order and as primary *causes* of escalating social problems, such as increasing crime rates, drug trafficking, prostitution, and inner-city decay.[5]

The complexity of social development among street children remains misconstrued.

The barrier that exists between abandoned children and adult cultures further motivates children's reliance on one another. Rather than use adults as role models, support and learned behavior develops in their relationships with other abandoned children. This experience of being raised by one's peers and in spite of adult intervention or negative influence creates a subculture of abandoned children only mildly understood and mainly feared by adults. Indeed, in the past, such a split between adult and child cultures has developed in Germany and been coined *"Kinderfeindlichkeit,"* which may be defined as "increasing anger at children who cannot or will not fulfill their expected roles in the transmission of 'traditional values.' "[6] The same hostility only toward abandoned children exists in Russia today.

Despite the seeming self sufficiency of Russia's street children, they cannot thrive without adult help. While there are moments when adult help seems undesirable, there is a need for adult intervention. This intervention must, however, occur with an understanding of the abandoned children themselves, the lives they live, and the appropriateness of the type of intervention. Adult intervention must be based on knowledge of the real needs and an idea of how it will help the children in the future. Historically, society's reaction to street children, fueled by a fear of them as antisocial and not quite human, involved institutionalization and extreme programs to eliminate their existence. In Brazil, for example, "organized 'death squads,' funded by the business community, frequently manned by off duty policemen,"[7] murdered street children as they slept in groups. While this is an extreme case, "severe social controls" continue to be in demand in urban areas across the world. In the end, such extreme initiatives have proven to be unsuccessful in eradicating the abandoned child issue. In fact, ripping children off the street and placing them into mismanaged institutions can do more harm than good. In the past, such intervention has lead to a larger rift between the children and the adult world, one that is based on mistrust and hatred.

One goal for adults working to heal abandoned children is to establish their trust and help them find love. For children who have become accustomed to making their own decisions on a daily basis in order to survive, robbing them of basic freedom will not result in friendship and trust. Controlling their lives means taking away their ability to know and understand their true needs. Rather, adult caretakers need to lead the children and intervene only when the children do not feel capable of making their own decisions. Adults need to show that they care in meaningful and consistent ways that make sense to the children as well.

Maria Osorina has suggested approaching all children carefully and with an understanding of their separateness and secret world. In her book on the secret lives of children, Osorina offers five categories for the educator. The first involves motivating and aiding children to achieve that which they fear. This involves acting as a role model for the child, showing her how she, too, can accomplish the seemingly impossible. In the case of abandoned children, these hurdles may be largely psychological.

Second, adults need to expand the horizons of children, telling and showing them their surrounding world and its potential. To the abandoned child, the world beyond their child culture, be it on the streets in gangs or in the institution, appears to be at war with the child. It is up to the adults to show the child how he, too, can succeed and find comfort in this apparent hostile environment.

The third category of intervention is to introduce the abandoned and street children to the natural environment. According to Osorina, "In particular the adult understands how important it is to experience nature in one's youth, to experience the landscapes, which touch the soul and call out a deep emotional response."[8] As an important aspect in Russian culture, the relationship of the environment to the soul is especially significant to the child's integration into Russian society and, perhaps more importantly, to his or her personal relationship with the surrounding environment and his or her sense of self.

Fourth, and perhaps even more important to an integration into Russian society, is the development of a sense of one's native country and of the homeland, a theme that permeates Russian culture. Osorina stresses its importance to every developing child:

The youth's quest for his personal identity—for the answer to the question "Who am I?"—unquestionably touches on the problem of ethnic and cultural self-determination and in part, on the identification of self amongst one's own people and one's own country . . . this understanding is necessary for the person's self understanding and for her future understanding of others.[9]

Osorina stresses that she is not suggesting blind patriotism or chauvinism, but a true understanding of one's past.

The final category of intervention is to teach the child his or her moral and ethical relationship to the surrounding world. For the abandoned child, this is perhaps one of the most difficult categories. Having been herself abused, neglected, and, in short, dealt with immorally, finding meaning in morality is difficult. And yet, without an understanding of good and bad, right or wrong, a child will not succeed in a society dominated by law. Children will only learn by observing and experiencing the right in the activities of their role models.[10]

Osorina, like many pioneering scholars of child culture, is coming to the conclusion that in order to help abandoned children, one must first acknowledge their independence from and significance to our adult world. Scholars of the future need to give a voice to children, be they abandoned or not.

Back in Russia again, I try to trace the footsteps of some of the children whom I met from the shelter and streets in Moscow: I cannot. Even Kolya, the boy with great hopes of being adopted in the United States, is nowhere to be found. Perhaps he has returned to his train station. Perhaps he has reunited with his brother and sister. Perhaps someone has taken him in. The chances of him living the life he dreamed of and came close to finding are slim. I look at his photograph and remember him at my house on Halloween, dressed up and going trick-or-treating with my boys. Those were happy moments yet they seem so minor considering all the hopes and dreams he held within himself at the time. All I can do now is hope that somehow he has found his home.

Appendix

U.S.-BASED ORGANIZATIONS

National Adoption Information Clearinghouse
330 C Street, SW
Washington, DC 20447
Tel.: 888-251-0075
http://naic.acf.hht.gov

This clearinghouse is a service of the Children's Bureau, Administration for Children and Families, U.S. Department of Health and Human Services. NAIC provides free information on all aspects of adoption.

Russian Children's Welfare Society
200 Park Avenue South
Suite 1617
New York, NY 10003
Tel.: 212-473-6263
http://www.rcws.org

This organization works to improve the lives of needy children of Russian descent in the world. RCWS provides grants to emigrant children and assists Russian children in their struggle against poverty.

Save the Children
  54 Wilton Road
  Westport, CT 06880
  Tel.: 203-221-4030
  http://www.savethechildren.org

This nonprofit child-assistance organization works in the United States and abroad in more than forty countries in the developing world to help children and families improve their health, education, and economic opportunities.

RUSSIA-BASED ORGANIZATIONS

Assistance to Russian Orphans
  Khokholovskii pereulok, d. 13, str.1
  109028 Moscow
  Tel.: 095-956-1400
  http://www.aro.ru

This program, funded and supported by USAID and IREX, works to protect and help orphans, children in crisis, and children with disabilities integrate into society and to foster political and regional reforms.

Goluba—Help Service for Girls
  Izmailovskoi shosse 55, kom. 67
  105187 Moscow
  Tel.: 095-369-0346

Goluba provides medical, psychological, and educational services and support for women under eighteen and their children.

Maria's Children
  Maria Yeliseyeva
  Dmitrovskii Pereulok 2/10
  Moscow, Russia
  Tel.: 095-292-4870
  http://www.mariaschildren.org

This Moscow-based organization provides art therapy and training for Russian orphans. The program offers an atmosphere in which children can recognize their creative potential, developing talents and self-esteem that will serve them in later life. By inviting these children into homes, teaching them life skills, and exposing them to safe, loving family environments, Maria Yeliseyeva hopes to improve the chances of successful integration into society.

Miramed Institute
Moscow, Russia
e-mail: raronson@miramed.org
office in US:
1900 West Nickerson, Suite 116
Seattle, WA 98119
Tel.: 206-285-0518
http://www.miramedinstitute.org

This public charity provides programs of social protection, education, training, and self-sufficiency for displaced and orphaned children in Russia and coalition-building, education, and training for the prevention of trafficking of girls and young women in Russia.

Notes

INTRODUCTION: ENTERING THE DOORWAY TO ABANDONED RUSSIA

1. U.S. Department of State 2003.
2. Ibid.
3. Maria at Maria's Children (interview) 2000.
4. Irina S. (interview) 1990.
5. Shweder and LeVine 1990, p. 69.
6. Rosenau 1992, p. 8.
7. Richmond 1992, p. 45.
8. Postman 1994, p. xi.
9. Ibid.
10. Ibid., p. xii.

CHAPTER 1: INSTITUTIONALIZED, NEGLECTED ORPHANS

1. Lahmeyer 2004, pp. 1–2.
2. Wachtel 1990, p. 2.
3. Galya T. (interview) 1992.
4. Tanya (interview) 1992.
5. Ibid.
6. Nina M. (interview) 1992.
7. Tanya M. (interview) 1992.

8. Human Rights Watch 1998, p. 9.

9. Ibid., p. 10.

10. Ibid., pp. 7–8.

11. Ibid.

CHAPTER 2: VICTIMS OF A FAILED SYSTEM, OR COLD CULTURAL BELIEFS?

1. Makarenko 1990, p. 253.

2. Mead and Wolfenstein 1955, p. 183.

3. Makarenko 1990, p. 55.

4. Pesmen 2000. The author agrees with Pesmen that one should speak of Russian soul as opposed to *the* Russian soul, as it does not represent one unilateral aspect of Russianness, but a complex that includes Russianness, Russian history, tradition, superstition, mysticism, philosophy, and emotion. See Pesmen, pp. 4–6.

5. Ibid., p. 16.

6. Ibid., p. 4.

7. Ibid., p. 267.

8. Ibid., p. 4.

9. Olga T. (interview) 2002.

10. Irina S. 1990.

11. Ibid.

12. Kennan in Richmond 1992, p. 44.

13. Tyutchev in Richmond 1992, p. 65. Translation amended by author.

14. Italics and definition inserted by author.

15. Dostoevsky in Ries 1997, p. 83.

16. Ries 1977, p. 83.

17. In fact, lamenting is a large part of everyday speech. Ries (1997) argues that lamenting or litany, as she labels it, can be analyzed as a communicative genre.

18. Ries 1997, p. 84.

19. Asya in *Age 7 in the USSR* (documentary) 1991.

20. Ries 1997, p. 87.

21. Ibid., p. 88.

22. Ibid., p. 111.

23. Tanya 1992.

24. Richmond 1992, pp. 90–92.

25. Dostoevsky 1993, pp. 34–35.

26. Nabokov in Katz 1991, p. 434.

27. Taxi driver (interview) 2000.

CHAPTER 3: MANY FORMS OF ABANDONMENT

1. Lena D. (interview) 1991.

2. Scheper-Hughes and Hoffman in Scheper-Hughes and Sargent 1998, p. 358.

3. Panter-Brick and Smith 2000, p. 140.

4. Ibid., p. 139.

5. Metcalf 2001, p. 167.

6. Panter-Brick and Smith 2000, p. 4.

7. Goffman 1963, p. 4.

8. Ibid.

9. Sapar Mulaevich (interview) 1999.

10. Goffman 1963, p. 5.

11. Ibid.

12. Scheper-Hughes and Hoffman in Scheper-Hughes and Sargent 1998, p. 357.

13. Ibid.

14. Panter-Brick and Smith 2000, p. 9.

15. Olga T. 2002.

16. Panter-Brick and Smith 2000, p. 7.

17. Hecht in Panter-Brick and Smith 2000, p. 154.

18. Ibid.

19. Ransel 1988, p. 8.

20. Ibid., p. 36.

21. Ibid., p. 125.

22. Ibid.

23. Ball 1994, p. 38.

24. Ibid., p. 64.

25. Ibid., p. 72.

26. Ibid., p. 83.

27. Ibid.

28. Ibid., p. 128.

29. Ibid., p. 195.

30. Ibid.

31. Ibid., p. 188.

32. Wachtel 1990, p. 2.

33. Tolstoy 1988, p. 7.
34. Ibid., p. 52.
35. Wachtel 1990, p. 2.
36. Ibid.
37. Ibid., p. 37.
38. Ibid., p. 54.
39. Terras 1985, p. 477.
40. Wachtel 1990, p. 3.
41. Ibid., pp. 4–5.
42. Ries 1977, p. 107.

CHAPTER 4: MOSCOW'S HOMELESS CHILDREN

1. Ball 1994, p. 63.
2. Ibid., p. 82.
3. Ibid.
4. Osorina 1999, pp. 156–157.
5. Ibid., p. 155.
6. McDonnell 1994, pp. 31–32.
7. Stoecker 2001, p. 320.
8. Ibid.
9. Ibid., p. 322.
10. Ibid.
11. Sapar Mulaevich 1999.
12. Bourdieu 1998, p. 43.
13. Oleg (interview) 1999–2001.
14. Metcalf 2001, p. 167.
15. Ibid.
16. Pesmen 2000, p. 135.
17. Stoecker 2001, p. 324.

CHAPTER 5: THE LURE OF THE CITY

1. Ferreira-Marques 2002, pp. 1–4.
2. Blanc 1994, p. 20.
3. Flowers 2001, p. 42.
4. Ibid.
5. Bushnell 1990, p. 229.
6. Ibid.

7. Ibid., pp. 230–231.
8. Ball 1995, p. 22.
9. DiMarco, Isaacs, Lord, and Seruya 2000, p. 21.
10. Ibid., pp. 21–22.
11. Ibid.
12. Ferreira-Marques 2002, p. 4.
13. Flowers 2001, p. 89.
14. UNAIDS 2002.
15. Zouev 1999, p. 28.
16. UNAIDS 2002.
17. Ibid.
18. Zouev 1999, p. 29.
19. Ibid., p. 28.
20. UNAIDS 2002.
21. Zouev 1999, p. 29.
22. Meier 2000.
23. Van Etten 2002, p. 3.
24. Olga 2000.
25. UNAIDS 2002.
26. Van Etten 2002, p. 1.
27. Meyer 2000, p. 1.
28. Blanc 1994, p. xv.
29. Flowers 2001, p. 47.
30. Blanc 1994, p. xv.
31. Ibid., p. xvi.

CHAPTER 6: DOMESTIC VIOLENCE CONTRIBUTING TO CHILD HOMELESSNESS

1. Sadovnikova 2001, p. 1.
2. Ibid.
3. Stoecker 2001, p. 323.
4. Matviyenko's figure on homeless children in Russia is conservative. The General Procuracy estimates 2 million, the Ministry of Internal Affairs (MVD) estimates 2.5 million, and the Federation Council estimates 3 million.
5. Matviyenko 2002, p. 176.
6. Mizulina 2002b, p. 5.
7. *Pathfinder on Domestic Violence* 1997, p. 14.
8. Gilinsky 2002.

9. Vetrova 1998, p. 96.
10. KDN 2002, p. 3.
11. Ibid.
12. Ibid.
13. Rossiiskaya Federatsiya 1999, p. 8.
14. Volkova 1996, p. 140.
15. PDN, OVD in Russian stands for *podrazdeleniye po delam nesover-shennoleynykh pravonarushitley, organy vnutrennykh del*—units dealing with juvenile offenders. Formerly, this unit was known as PPPN—*podrazdeleniye po profilaktike nesovershennykh pravonarushitelei.*
16. Sotsial'naya rabota 2000.
17. Stoecker 1996, p. 5.
18. Kerner 1998, p. 165.
19. Revin 1996, p. 21.
20. Veklenko and Volkova 1996, p. 72.
21. RIA Novosti 2002.

CHAPTER 7: OPTIONS FOR THE ABANDONED CHILD

1. International League for Human Rights 1998, pp. 3–16.
2. Glasser 2002, p. 18.
3. Ibid.
4. Olga T. 2002.
5. Ibid.
6. Aleksei (interview) 2003.
7. Ibid.
8. ITAR-TASS 1999.
9. Boris (interview) 1994.
10. *Gosha* (documentary) 1993.
11. Bernstein 1995, p. 3.
12. Ibid.
13. Ibid.
14. Ling 1997, p. 1.
15. Susak 2000, p. 1.
16. Caldwell 1997, p. 1.
17. Specter 1998, p. 3.
18. Kirill 1994.
19. Amnesty International 2002a.
20. Gilgen and Gilgen in Koltsova et al. 1996, p. 7.

21. Ibid., p. 38.
22. Joravsky 1989, p. 314.
23. Ibid.
24. Brenner 1999, p. 9.
25. Maria 2000.
26. Bureau of Consular Affairs 2005.
27. National Adoption Information Clearinghouse 2004.
28. Ruark 2002, p. A12.
29. Ibid.
30. Ibid.
31. Harris 1995, p. 281.
32. Ibid.
33. Lisa Palmer (interview) 2002.
34. Ibid.
35. Jane (interview) 1999–2000.
36. Lisa Palmer 2002.
37. Maria 2000.
38. Lisa Palmer 2002.

CONCLUSION: THEIR WORLD STILL WITH SECRETS AND SORROW

1. Friedl 2002, p. 19.
2. Hirschfeld 2002, p. 612.
3. Ibid.
4. Osorina 1999, p. 8.
5. Stephens 1995, p. 12.
6. Ibid., p. 9.
7. Ibid., p. 12.
8. Osorina 1999, p. 276.
9. Ibid.
10. Ibid., pp. 273–277.

Bibliography

PUBLISHED TEXTS

Abel'tsev, S. (1995). *Semeyinye konflikty i prestupleniye*. Moscow: Rossi-iskaya iustitsy.

Aries, P. (1962). *Centuries of Childhood: A Social History of Family Life*. New York: Vintage Books.

Armitage, R. (2000). *Family Violence*. Austin, TX: Raintree Steck-Vaughn.

Baker, P. (2001). "Vodka's Place in the Russian Soul." *Washington Post*, July 2: A11.

Ball, A. (1994). *And Now My Soul Is Hardened: Abandoned Children in Soviet Russia, 1918–1930*. Berkeley: University of California Press.

Bernstein, L. (1995). *Sonia's Daughters: Prostitutes and Their Regulation in Imperial Russia*. Berkeley: University of California Press.

Blanc, C. (1994). *Urban Children in Distress: Global and Innovative Strategies*. Florence, Italy: United Nations Children's Fund.

Bourdieu, P. (1998). *Acts of Resistance: Against the Tyranny of the Market*. New York: New York Press.

Bushnell, J. (1990). *Moscow Graffiti: Language and Subculture*. Boston: Unwin Hyman.

Caldwell, G. (1997). "Crime and Servitude." Washington, DC: Global Survival Network.

Chukovsky, K. (1968). *From Two to Five*. Berkeley: University of California Press.

Cornia, A., and S. Sipos, eds. (1991). *Children and the Transition to the Market Economy*. Aldershot, UK: Avebury.

Creuziger, C. (1996). *Childhood in Russia: Representation and Reality*. Lanham, MD: University Press of America.

———. (1997). "Russia's Unwanted Children: A Cultural Anthropological Study of Marginalized Children in Moscow and St. Petersburg." *Childhood* 4, no. 3: 343–359.

Dement'eva, I. (1992). *Sotsial'nye problemy sirotstva*. Moscow: Rossiiskaya Adademiya Nauk, Institut Sotsiologii.

Dostoevsky, F. (1993). *Notes from the Underground*. Reprint, New York: Vintage Books. Originally published in 1864.

Feshbach, M. (1995). *Ecological Disaster: Cleaning Up the Hidden Legacy of the Soviet Regime*. New York: Twentieth Century Fund Press.

Flowers, R. B. (2001). *Runaway Kids and Teenage Prostitution: America's Lost, Abandoned, and Sexually Exploited Children*. Westport, CT: Praeger.

Friedl, E. (2002). "Why Are Children Missing from Textbooks?" *Anthropology News* (May): 19.

Geertz, C. (1973). *Interpretation of Cultures*. New York: Basic Books.

Gilinsky, Y. I. (2002). *Kriminologiya*. St. Petersburg: Piter.

Glasser, S. (2002). "Deserting Russia's Desparate Army." *Washington Post*, September 20: A1, A18.

Goffman, E. (1963). *Stigma: Notes on the Management of Spoiled Identity*. New York: Simon and Schuster.

Harris, J. (1998). *The Nurture Assumption: Why Children Turn Out the Way They Do*. New York: Free Press.

Harris, M. (1995). *Introduction to Anthropology*. New York: Cambridge University Press.

Harvard Health Publications. (2000). "The Mortality of Men in Russia: A Cautionary Tale." *Reinsurance Notes* 2, no. 4 (March): 5–6.

Hirschfeld, L. A. (2002). "Why Don't Anthropologists Like Children?" *American Anthropologist* 104, no. 2: 611–627.

Joravsky, D. (1989). *Russian Psychology: A Critical History*. Oxford, UK: Basil Blackwell.

Katz, M. (1991). *Tolstoy's Short Fiction*. New York: W. W. Norton.

Kerner, K., ed. (1998). *Kriminologiya. Slovar'-spravochnik*. Moscow: Progress Publishers.

Koltsova, V. A., Y. N. Oleinik, A. R. Gilgen, and C. K. Gilgen, eds. (1996). *Post-Soviet Perspectives on Russian Psychology*. Westport, CT: Greenwood Press.

Kudriyatseva, V. N., and A. V. Naumova. (1997). *Nasil'stvennaya prestup-nost'*. Moscow: Spark.

Ling, C. (1997). "Rights Activists Rap Ex-Soviet States on Sex-Trade." *Reuters*, November 6: 1.

Makarenko, A. (1990). *Selected Pedagogical Works*. Moscow: Progress Publishers.

Matviyenko, V. (2002). "Detskaya besprizornost' i beznadzornost': problemy, puti resheniya." *Analitichesky vestnik Soveta Federatsy* [Moscow], no. 20.

McDonnell, K. (1994). *Kid Culture: Children and Adults and Popular Culture*. Toronto: Second Story Press.

Mead, M., and M. Wolfenstein, eds. (1955). *Childhood in Contemporary Russia*. Chicago: University of Chicago Press.

Metcalf, P. (2001). "'Global Disjuncture' and the Sites of Anthropology." *Cultural Anthropology* 16, no. 2: 167.

Mizulina, E. (2002a). "Poteryavshiesia sredi nas." *Rossiya* 4, no. 277 (January 31–February 6).

———. (2002b). "*O dopolnitel'nykh merakh po usileniyu bor'by s beznadzornostyu i besprizornosyu nesovershennoletnykh.*" *Analitichesky otchet mezhvedomstvennoy komissy po delam nesovershennoletnykh i zashchite ikh prav*. Irkutsk: Irkutsk Publishing House.

Opie, I., and P. Opie. (1969). *Children's Games in Street and Playground*. Oxford, UK: Clarendon Press.

Osorina, M. (1999). *Sekretnyi mir detei v prostranstve mira vzroslykh*. St. Petersburg: Piter.

Panter-Brick, C., and M. Smith, eds. (2000). *Abandoned Children*. Cambridge, UK: Cambridge University Press.

Pathfinder on Domestic Violence in the United States. (1997). New York: Center on Crime, Communities, and Culture.

Pertman, A. (2000). *Adoption Nation: How the Adoption Revolution Is Transforming America*. New York: Basic Books.

Pesmen, D. (2000). *Russia and Soul: An Exploration*. Ithaca, NY: Cornell University Press.

Postman, N. (1994). *The Disappearance of Childhood*. New York: Vintage Books.

Puzankov, V. (1990). *Anton Makarenko: Selected Pedagogical Works*. Moscow: Progress Publishers.

Ransel, D. (1988). *Mothers of Misery: Child Abandonment in Russia*. Princeton, NJ: Princeton University Press.

Revin, V. P. (1996). *Kriminal'noe nasilie v sferakh sem'i, byta, dosuga:*

sotsial'no-pravovye problemy bor'by s nasiliem. Omsk: Omsk State Technical University Publishers.

Richmond, Y. (1992). *From Nyet to Da: Understanding the Russians.* Yarmouth, ME: Intercultural Press, Inc.

Ries, N. (1997). *Russian Talk: Culture and Conversation During Perestroika.* Ithaca, NY: Cornell University Press.

Rivman, D. V., and V. S. Ustinov. (2000). *Viktimologiya.* St. Petersburg: Iuridicheskii Tsentr Press.

Rosenau, P. M. (1992). *Post-Modernism and the Social Sciences: Insights, Inroads, and Intrusions.* Princeton, NJ: Princeton University Press.

Ruark, J. (2002). "What Makes a Family? A Historian Traces the Rise and Fall of Adoption in America." *Chronicle of Higher Education* 49, no. 9: A12.

Sadovnikova, M. N. (2000). *Sotsial'naya rabota s nesovershennoletnymi. Opyt organizatsy sotsial'noy sluzhby.* Moscow: Progress Publishers.

———. (2001). *Prava podrostkov i mekhanizmy ikh zashchity.* Irkutsk: Publishing House of Irkutsk University.

Sapir, E. (1949). "The Emergence of the Concept of Personality in a Study of Cultures." In *Selected Writings in Language, Culture, and Personality,* David G. Mandelbaum, ed. (pp. 590–597). Berkeley: University of California Press.

Scheper-Hughes, N. (1992). *Death without Weeping: The Violence of Everyday Life in Brazil.* Berkeley: University of California Press.

Scheper-Hughes, N., and C. Sargent, eds. (1998). *Small Wars: The Cultural Politics of Childhood.* Berkeley: University of California Press.

Schwartzman, H. (1978). *Transformations: The Anthropology of Children's Play.* New York: Plenum Press.

Shweder, R., and R. LeVine, eds. (1990). *Culture Theory: Essays on Mind, Self, and Emotion.* New York: Cambridge University Press.

Slater, S. (1995). *The Lesbian Family Life Cycle.* New York: Free Press.

Stephens, S., ed. (1995). *Children and the Politics of Culture.* Princeton, NJ: Princeton University Press.

Stoecker, S. W. (1996). *Ugolovnyi kodeks Rossiiskoy Federatsy.* St. Petersburg: Alfa.

———. (2001). "Homelessness and Criminal Exploitation of Russian Minors: Realities, Resources and Legal Remedies." *Demokratizatsiya: The Journal of Post-Soviet Democratization* 9, no. 2 (Spring): 319–336.

Tolstoy, L. (1988). *Childhood, Boyhood, Youth.* Reprint, New York: Penguin Books. Originally published in 1852.

Veklenko, S. V., and A. E. Volkova. (1996). *Kriminogennost' zhestokogo obrashcheniya s det'mi.* Omsk: Omsk State Technical University Publishers.

Vetrova, N. I., and Yu. I. Lyapunov. (2000). *Ugolovnoe pravo: osobennaia chast': uchebnik.* Moscow: Zakon i pravo.

Virtanen, L. (1978). *Children's Lore.* Helsinki: Studia Fennica, Finnish Literary Society.

Volkova, A. E. (1996). *Zhesokost' i nasilie kak kriminologicheskaya problema: sotsial'no-pravovye problemy bor'by s nasiliem.* Omsk: Omsk State Technical University Publishers.

Wachtel, A. (1990). *The Battle for Childhood: Creation of a Russian Myth.* Stanford, CA: Stanford University Press.

Waggenspack, B. (1998). "The Symbolic Crisis of Adoption: Popular Media's Agenda-Setting." *Adoption Quarterly* 1, no. 4: 57–82.

Whiting, B., and J. Whiting, eds. (1966). *Field Guide for a Study of Socialization.* New York: John Wiley and Sons.

Zouev, A., ed. (1999). *Generation in Jeopardy: Children in Central and Eastern Europe and the Former Soviet Union.* Armonk, NY: M.E. Sharpe.

PRIMARY SOURCES

Akty sudebno-psikhiyatricheskikh ekspertiz, suda Irkutskogo goroda i Irkutskoy oblasti, 1997–2002. [Legal documentation by the city of Irkutsk on psychiatric cases.]

Arkhiv oblastnogo suda Irkutskoy oblasti za 1997–2002. [Irkutsk legal archive.]

KDN (Komissiya po delam nesovershennoletnymi). [Irkutsk City and Oblast, reports on child homelessness and juvenile crime, 2002–2003.]

Rossiiskaya Federatsiya, Federal'nyi zakon "ob osnovakh sistemy profilaktiki beznadzornosti i pravonarushenyi nesovershennoletnykh." Adopted on June 9, 1999, *Sbornik federal'nykh konstitutsionnykh i federal'nykh zakonov Rossiiskoy Federatsii, vypusk* 12(84). [A compilation of Russia's federal constitution and laws.]

WEB DOCUMENTS

Amnesty International. (2002a). "Urgent Action Needed to Combat Disease in Russia's Prisons" (press release). www.amnesty.org.uk/justice forallinrussia/action/tb/pressrelease.shtml. Accessed March 14, 2004.

————. (2002b). "The Treatment of Children in Custody and Detention." www.amnestyusa.org/countries/russia/campaign/ children_detention .html. Accessed October 28, 2004.

Brenner, F. (1999). "Intrepid Thought: Psychoanalysis in the Soviet Union— Part 2." World Socialist Web Site, www.wsws.org/articles/1999/ jun1999/freu-j12.shtml. Accessed June 30, 2003.

Bureau of Consular Affairs, U.S. Department of State. (2005). "U.S. Immigrant Visa Statistics." http://travel.state.gov/family/adoption/stats/ stats_451.html. Accessed May 30, 2005.

DiMarco, B., A. Isaacs, J. Lord, and A. Seruya. (2000). "Children's Health in Russia." *Childhood around the World.* www.tulane.edu/~rouxbee/ kids00/russia4.html. Accessed December 8, 2003.

Ferreira-Marques, C. (2002). "Russia: Moscow's Street Children Struggle to Survive." *Reuters*, February 28, www.ripnet.org/strategies/manifestevil/ rmscsts.htm. Accessed January 25, 2003.

Human Rights Watch. (1998). "Abandoned to the State: Cruelty and Neglect in Russian Orphanages." http://hrw.org/reports98/russia2/. Accessed December 1, 2003.

International League for Human Rights League Reports. "Implementation of the Convention on the Rights of the Child." http://www.ilhr.org/ ilhr/reports/children/. Accessed July 3, 2004.

ITAR-TASS. (1999). "Juvenile Delinquency Rate on the Rise in Russia," November 30. www.cdi.org/russia/johnson/3654.html. Accessed May 30, 2005.

Johnson, D. (2003). "The Criminal Economy: The Structure of Prostitution." *Johnson's Russia List*, www.cdi.org/russia/johnson/7069-6 .cfm. Accessed November 25, 2004.

Lahmeyer, J. (2004). "Pupulstat" site, University Utrecht, Netherlands. www.library.uu.nl/wesp/populstat/Europe/russiag.htm. Accessed January 1, 2004.

Maria's Children. (2003). www.mariaschildren.com. Accessed September 10, 2003.

Meier, A. (2000). "Tuberculosis: The Age of Consumption." *Time Europe*, January 22, www.time.come/time/europe/magazine/2001/0122/ cover_tb.html. Accessed June 6, 2004.

Meyer, H. (2000). "Russia-AIDS Drugs." AFP, December 18, www.aegis .com/news/afp/2000/Af001283.html. Accessed December 18, 2000.

National Adoption Information Clearinghouse. (2004). "Fact About Adoption." http.//naic.acf.hhs.gov/pubs/s_adoptedhighlights.cfm. Accessed May 30, 2005.

RFE/RL Newsline, 29 March, (Un)Civil Societies, 2, no. 14. www.ripnet
.org/strategies/manifestevil/rypcocit.htm. Accessed June 6, 2004.

Specter, M. (1998). "Traffickers' New Cargo: Native Slavic Women." *New
York Times*, January 11. www.ukar.org/specter01.html. Accessed
January 11, 1998.

Susak, I. (2000). "Slavery Today." *CSIS Prospectus* 1, no. 2 (Summer).
www.csis.org/pubs/prospectus/00summerSusak.html. Accessed May
1, 2000.

Truth in Media Bulletin. (2000). www.truthinmedia.org, October 14. pp.
2–11. Accessed November 1, 2000.

UNAIDS. (2002). "Fact Sheet: HIV/AIDS in Eastern Europe, Central Asia."
U.S. Department of State International Programs, United Nations.
http://usinfo.state.gov/topical/global/hiv/02070304.htm. Accessed July
3, 2000.

U.S. Department of State. (2003). "Country Reports on Human Rights Practices: Russia." www.state.gov/g/drl/rls/hrrpt/2003/27861pf/htm. Accessed February 25, 2004.

Van Etten, B. (2002). "Russia Fights Increase of AIDS Victims." Voice
of America. www.voanews.com/english/Archive/a-2002-11-06-50-
Russia.cfm. Accessed November 6, 2002.

Weir, F. (2001). "Russia: Runaways Find Few Willing to Help Them."
Christian Science Monitor, www.ripnet.org/strategies/manifestevil/
rrffwtht.htm. Accessed December 19, 2004.

FILMS

Dokuchaev, Y. (1993). *Gosha* (documentary). Moscow, Wide Angle Pictures.

Lawrence, S., and S. Miroshnichenko. (1991). *Age 7 in the USSR* (documentary). Moscow, Grenada Television.

INTERVIEWS

Aleksei, émigré, Annapolis, MD, winter 2003.

Boris, business owner, Moscow, summer 1994.

Dmitrii, orphanage resident, age fifteen, St. Petersburg, fall 1990.

G. Family, Annapolis, MD, 2003.

Galya T., orphan teacher, Moscow, summer 1992.

Irina S., teacher and professor of education, Gertzen University, St. Petersburg, fall 1990.

Jane, mother of adopted girl, Moscow and United States, 1999–2000.

Katya, orphan, age eighteen, Moscow, winter 1999.

Kirill, ex-convict, Moscow, summer 1994.

Kolya, homeless boy, age twelve, Moscow, winter 2000.

Lena D., Leningrad blockade survivor, spring 1991.

Maria, Maria's Children director, Moscow, winter 2000.

Masha, orphan, age twelve, Moscow, summer 1994.

Nina M., orphanage pediatrician, Moscow, summer 1992.

Oleg, worker, Moscow, 1999–2001.

Olga T., mother and editor, Moscow, spring 2002.

Palmer Family, Moscow and Iowa, 2000–2003.

Pasha, shelter resident, age ten, St. Petersburg, October 1990.

Sapar Mulaevich, Way Home shelter director, Moscow, fall and winter 1999.

Tanya, orphan caretaker, Moscow, summer 1992.

Tanya M., orphan, age five, Moscow, summer 1992.

Taxi driver, Moscow, winter 2000.

Index

About the Author and Contributors

CLEMENTINE K. FUJIMURA is an Associate Professor of language and culture studies at the United States Naval Academy, where she teaches Russian and German, culture, and literature courses. She received her doctorate in cultural anthropology from the University of Chicago and has been writing about Russia's homeless children, abandonment, and its cultural concept of childhood since 1991. She has received numerous grants and fellowships in support of her work on homeless children in Russia.

SALLY W. STOECKER is a Lecturer in ciminology and criminal law, and a candidate of sciences, at Baikal State University of Economics in Irkutsk, Russia. Her research focuses on child homelessness, drug addiction of minors, and juvenile crime. She is formerly Coordinator of the Irkutsk Center for the Study of Organized Crime and Corruption in Irkutsk.

TATYANA SUDAKOVA is Scholar-in-Residence at American University's Transnational Crime and Corruption Center (TraCCC), where she conducts research on human trafficking, child homelessness and exploitation, and juvenile crime. Stoecker also teaches courses on child homelessness and exploitation, and juvenile crime. Stoecker teaches courses on Russian politics in the School of International Service at American University and served as Executive Editor of *Demokratizatsiya: The Journal of Post-Soviet Democratization* for six years.